The Down and
Dirty Dish on
REVENGE

The Down and Dirty Dish on

REVENGE

Serving It Up
Nice and Cold
to That Lying,
Cheating Bastard

Eva Nagorski

Thomas Dunne Books
St. Martin's Griffin ✳ New York

THOMAS DUNNE BOOKS.

An imprint of St. Martin's Press.

THE DOWN AND DIRTY DISH ON REVENGE. Copyright © 2009 by Eva Nagorski.
Illustrations copyright © 2009 by Michael Lotenero. All rights reserved.
Printed in the United States of America. For information, address St. Martin's Press,
175 Fifth Avenue, New York, N.Y. 10010.

www.thomasdunnebooks.com

www.stmartins.com

Library of Congress Cataloging-in-Publication Data

Nagorski, Eva.
    The down and dirty dish on revenge : serving it up nice and cold to
that lying, cheating bastard / Eva Nagorski. — 1st ed.
        p. cm.
    ISBN-13: 978-0-312-37957-5
    ISBN-10: 0-312-37957-9
  1. Revenge.   I. Title.
    BF637.R48.N64 2009
    306.73'6—dc22   2009009630

First Edition: June 2009

10 9 8 7 6 5 4 3 2 1

For my husband, Taylor,
So that the R word between us is always Romance
And with whom I share our very own Caye

Author's Note

Names that have been changed are first used in quotation marks. This book is intended to inform and entertain; it is not meant as an instructive guide. Readers who consider undertaking any actions similar to those described in this book should first consult professional legal counsel about possible adverse consequences. The fact that an organization or Web site is referred to as a source of information does not mean that the author endorses the information the organization or Web site may provide or the recommendations it may make. Further, readers should be aware that Web sites may have changed or disappeared between when this book was written and when it is read.

Contents

Acknowledgments

When Deep Focus hired me to write the "That Girl Emily" blog for the Court TV promotional campaign for the TV show *Parco PI,* I figured it'd be a fun ride, but I had no idea it'd pave the way for a book. So a big shout-out to Ian Schafer, Jim Marsh, Sabrina Calouri, and Jason Valentzas for bringing me on board.

Huge props to my agent, Andrea Somberg, who encouraged me to put the idea of a passionate revenge book on paper; she has far exceeded my expectations with all of her tireless hard work, support, and wine! I couldn't ask for a better person to represent me.

A big thank-you to Thomas Dunne for publishing this book, and specifically to my editor, Toni Plummer, who did a superb job shaping it. And to Michael Lotenero, the book's illustrator, who effortlessly churned out hilarious art on such a "dark" subject.

I have many others to thank who took the time to give me fodder for my book, including Gary S. DeFinis, who let me peek into his private investigator world—thanks to an introduction by Cici McNair. There were many others who helped me virtually. In particular, I'd like to mention Nick James, the founder of www.getrevengeonyourex.com, who died unexpectedly at such a young age. He generously spread the word that I was seeking stories, and candidly shared his own tales, thoughts, and theories.

Thank you to all of the experts and professors who offered their invaluable advice and perspectives: Vinny Parco, Susan Boon, David Buss, Raymond DiGiuseppe, Steven Hodes, Kristina Coop Gordon, David Sbarra, Tom Smith, and Stephen M. Yoshimura. And to those who led me to them, especially Sara Bailey Nagorski and Heidi Kane.

Then there are all the personalities who gave me quotes for my book: Louis Begley, Nigel Cawthorne, Bruce Jay Friedman, Janusz Glowacki, Melissa Joan Hart, Agnieszka Holland, Shar Jackson, Stacy Keach, Tina Louise, and Nile Rodgers.

Of course, this book would not be what it is without all the people who contributed their personal stories of revenge. Although they remain nameless in the book, they all deserve credit for sharing so honestly, openly, and even enthusiastically. I appreciate them reminding us that revenge is a very real and human aspect of everyday life.

There are so many others to thank. Specifically: my grandparents Marie and Zyg Nagorski, for their unfailing support; the friends who helped in any way they could—Tiffany Bartok, Ania Bogusz, Davide Butson, Carla Capretto, Heather Florence, Diana Frost, Josh Gaspero, Zoe Gensel, Jenny Gering, Sandra and Patty Goldman, Nancy Hunt, Violetta Klimczewska, Shola Lynch, Clara Markowicz, Diane Paragas, Sooze Plunkett-Green, Charles and Kelly Poe, Matt Pyken and Dyanne Chae, Karen Quinn, Robynn Ragland, Jen Senko,

Francine Shane, Adam Wierzbianski, Tomasz Zorawski, and many others; Russell and Peggy Green; my mother-in-law, Lowry Marshall; and my remarkable siblings: Sonia, Adam, and Alex.

Lastly, five people who are so dear to me and to whom I owe so much:

Agatha Dominik, who is in a class all of her own when it comes to being a friend, editor, supporter, and confidante. She truly goes above and beyond.

My parents, Andrew and Christina Nagorski, the best friends a daughter can have. Their unwavering and unconditional support, and ability to always make time for me even when they have no time left, has been invaluable throughout my life. They've been my inspiration from day one.

To say my gorgeous daughter, Caye, was part of the writing process is an understatement. While I was writing this book, she was growing inside of me. When my editor handed me her first round of editing queries, she popped out. Then I was alternating between nursing her and making final editorial fixes on the book. Every day Caye makes me feel like an incredibly lucky person.

So does Caye's father, my husband and my love, Taylor Marshall-Green. One of his wedding vows was to never tell me my writing was good when it wasn't. He not only has stayed true to that, he also inspires me with his zest, humor, and tremendous talent with words. "Grateful" doesn't come close to describing how I feel about what he's done and continues to do. Not just in writing, but in making our life together simply—and on every complex level—delicious.

The Down and
Dirty Dish on
REVENGE

Introduction

Let's cut to the chase.

After a long, arduous day at the office, you return home to find your husband gagged and being spanked with a cane by some goth chick smoking a cigar and reciting the poetry of e.e. cummings. Needless to say, they expected you much later.

Your boyfriend has been putting off marriage for three years and recently told you that he wants to be single again. All of this information was administered via text message. WTF?!

You put your husband through law school on your measly waitress salary, pulling more double shifts than that century-old restaurant had ever recalled. But he kept saying he wasn't ready for kids. Recently, he *schtupped* some fashion designer wannabe who's ten years younger than you, decided it was over between you two, and handed you divorce papers. That skinny lil' bitch is now pregnant with twins.

So, do you feel "it" yet? "It" being the unmistakable pain of being cheated on, lied to, or dumped. It's a feeling you wish would go away. You've found yourself in a disgusting state: splayed on the couch with bits of Häagen-Dazs Coffee and Almond Crunch melted into your cashmere sweater and ginger cookie crumbs caught in your zipper. Basically, you've turned into a pathetic bag of bitter skin and self-hating congestion.

But then, as time moves on, the pain does begin to go away—or rather, turn into something else, a different emotion, a different intangible. An incredible transformation of nature takes place, like a moth emerging from a chrysalis. Your bitter skin hardens, your congestion from crying turns into snarls, and your mind begins to swirl. Suddenly, food begins to taste better. You see, hear, and focus on things you've never seen, heard, or focused on before: the evening news anchorman's jawline, birds singing in the dusk, a rug in your house. You start to forget about the good times you had with your lover or husband, and begin reliving the bad times over and over again. The remnants of his things that he's planned to pick up no longer make you sad; instead, they begin taunting you, regardless of how small they are: his hair still clinging to the white bar of soap, his chocolate syrup loitering in the fridge, his wet suit hanging in the garage.

You begin to feel scorn. It transforms into hate. And then, with a rush, you experience an epiphany. You see a vision in your mind: your ex suffering just like you have, feeling what you've felt, getting what you've gotten. And the sinister serum of vengeance floods into your bloodstream from an undiscovered reservoir located somewhere between your left ventricle and your medulla. We'll call it the "retaliation gland."

You start thinking about how tomorrow doesn't look so cloudy anymore, about how tomorrow is going to be different for you. You're ready to move on, but first, you have a couple of *i*'s to dot and some *t*'s to cross. You have a favor to repay. Thinking about it makes you angry but it also makes you hungry. Hungry for revenge.

This will be your fully loaded, maxed-out, juiced-up book on how people devise, execute, and relish revenge. If revenge were a martial art, this book would be your dojo and the pages your sensei. If revenge were an automobile, you'd be currently reading the manual. If revenge were a casserole, this would be your recipe book.

Sure, there are those who heed the Latin proverb "Revenge is a confession of pain." Well, those people can bite me. This is the kind of Latin I can groove with: *"Aut vincere aut mori."* Either conquer or die.

This book will let you live vicariously through people who have experienced exacting intoxicating, imaginative, and cold revenge. It will also dissect, investigate, and apply "revenge" historically, anecdotally, and comically. Samuel Beckett wrote in his play *Endgame*, "Nothing is funnier than unhappiness." Let's see who's laughing now.

I once was involved in revenge. But mine was purely vicarious. In 2006, I was hired by the advertising company Deep Focus to write the blog "That Girl Emily," part of Court TV's highly successful and award-winning marketing campaign for their television program *Parco PI*.

The fictional Emily, a typical suburban wife, found out that her husband was cheating on her. So instead of taking it lying down, she declared on her blog "14 Days of Wrath," targeting her husband. On the first day, she announced that she would tell the whole world about his infidelity and paltry sexual equipment by taking out billboard ads in New York and Los Angeles that said:

> Hi Steven,
>> Do I have your attention now?
>> I know all about her, you dirty, sneaky, immoral, unfaithful, poorly endowed slimeball. Everything's caught on tape.
>> Your (soon-to-be-ex) Wife,
> Emily
>
> p.s. I paid for this billboard from OUR joint bank account.

People would stand mystified in the middle of Times Square, staring at the billboard, amazed and intrigued that some scorned woman would have the ovaries to do that to her husband. Cell-phone photos were spread across cyberspace, and the marketing campaign erupted in all its viral glory to e-mail accounts everywhere in the world.

Within two weeks, more than two million people had clicked onto Emily's blog. The support for her cause was simply awesome. Countless e-mails, from South Carolina to Sweden, Iceland to Indonesia, Russia to Rome, came pouring in, proclaiming that Emily had inspired them, was their hero, and had given them the strength to get through their own similar heartbreak. Radio and television stations wanted interviews with Emily; women wanted advice, men wanted dates. Husbands and wives would admit sitting together with their coffee and pouring over Emily's blog every morning. It was surprising to see the number of men who wrote to sympathize with Emily, saying that they, too, had been cheated on and hurt.

There were those who were angry or felt duped when they found out that Emily wasn't a real person. But on the whole, even those who found out she was make-believe continued to read Emily's blog and show support for her. "Emily is really an amalgam of all of us who have been cheated on," Marc Juris, general manager for programming and marketing at Court TV at the time, told *The New York Times*. "Clearly, this really resonated with people."

What was the trick to making this campaign so successful? "A meme of revenge was really starting to pick up steam at that time," says Ian Schafer, CEO of Deep Focus, the advertising company behind the campaign. "What was happening was YouTube's explosion onto the scene . . . There was an explosion of videos that girlfriends would make for their boyfriends, usually involving some kind of striptease, then [the relationship] ends in some kind of nasty breakup and the next thing that happens, the videotape is being circulated, then it's being uploaded into some kind of file-sharing service. Documenting breakups, documenting incidents of revenge, has really become normal. I think more and more what's happening is that any kind of veil of privacy between two individuals has pretty much been lifted."

Jim Marsh, an account executive at Deep Focus during the campaign, confirmed this by saying that the campaign was a success "because it followed one of the most important rules of advertising—appeal to people's emotions. This particular campaign focused on a subject that hits close to home for so many people: infidelity. Everyone who has been hurt by a significant other knows that the desire to get even can be overwhelming. Emily was created as a champion of this cause."

And it worked. Emily became an instant icon for revenge.

T-shirts were made. Emily's videos and photos of her 14 Days of Wrath were viewed all over the world. Readers even began saying that if they ever caught their lover cheating, they'd "Emily" them! And the blog is still up, years later, as I am writing this, and may still be up when you are reading this book today. Emily became the modern urban legend of a woman scorned. Publishers even wrote, requesting the rights to her story.

"[Revenge] is a frequent storyline in TV shows and films, and it's something we like to draw on," says Schafer. "Because whether you've taken revenge on somebody or not, at some point in time, you've evaluated the consequences of doing so, and sometimes the road not taken works best when it comes to advertising because it lets people have someone else experience it for them."

This book isn't an advertising campaign. But its mission is to let you experience revenge in every possible way—all within the "friendly confines" of this here book!

So let's start with the basics. In order to exact revenge, one must first prove that revenge is warranted. Just because you found two movie stubs in his pocket for a film you never saw doesn't mean you should fill his golf bag with cement. Within these pages, you'll read about those lost and misguided souls who dished out payback without doing their homework. We'll dissect what happens when you've jumped the gun by moving forward with vengeful plans without making sure you have concrete evidence. Your boyfriend has been sneaking around suspiciously, so you slash his tires, only to find out he was organizing a surprise birthday party for you. These impulsive actions can backfire quickly and really put a damper on the birthday party *and* your love life.

From suspect receipts to home videos left in the VCR, Chapter 1 will help you see the hints, signals, and warnings that your marriage or relationship is heading toward . . . well, the shitter.

Now, in order to gear up for some serious revenge, you may need to take a little inspiration from history. We'll set the "way-back" machine to the beginning of time, when wives would paint "cheater" on a man's camel or donkey. We'll also look at how ex-lovers and -spouses were punished by their governments with laws and codes against cheating and other unacceptable extramarital behavior. Think Hammurabi; think Draconian; think castration.

When done legally and without physical harm, revenge can be healthier and more affordable than eating a pound of chocolate, liquidating your 401(k)s, or paying a therapist for aloe-laced tissues. Revenge can be a way to bring back your own feelings of self-worth, dignity, and justice. But don't get me wrong—revenge can also land you in the slammer.

This will be your sidekick while doing a little voyeuristic sightseeing of no-holds-barred revenge. If you want to go beyond the voyeur, make sure everything is fair, justified, and legal. (*Is sending porn to my ex-husband's parents legal? Can I smash the back window of his Audi if we're both on the title? Oops, I accidentally dropped laxatives in his morning coffee—can he prove anything?*)

There will also be a section devoted to what can be done with advanced technology. The Digital Age has made forming, nurturing, and ending relationships relatively simple. But for the truly obsessive, it's also made it much easier to keep track of an ex's subsequent relationships—and then find ways to make him pay for those post-breakup "infidelities." One click of the mouse and your ex-husband could be the proud new owner of an African white rhino (nonrefundable).

Despite the countless stories and methods detailed here, some people may wonder if they're insane or just plain sinners for wishing revenge on an ex. We'll take the guesswork out of it for you. According to some psychoanalysts, revenge can be explored as a chemical reaction or even a sociopath state. Is revenge literally in your blood? Is it passed down from your mother? Can you receive treatment for this "condition"? Writers and other reputable personalities have focused on revenge for centuries. Here, several famous personalities reveal their own firsthand take on revenge. It is an emotion most people have at least sensed momentarily. It's also a stark reminder that we're all human.

It's also good to remember that when a guy cheats once, he'll probably cheat again, no matter who he's with, what he looks like, or what he tells you. That means that the woman he's shagging isn't necessarily the enemy. She'll get hers in due time, so you should be sensitive when it comes to making her pay as well. That is, unless it's your sister or your best friend. Surely, make them pay.

You will also notice that although this book is geared toward a female audience, there will be plenty of stories by men who were cheated on or lied to and exacted their own revenge. It's good to look at the other side of the coin—and usually, the revenge options are not gender-specific anyway.

Now is the time to look deep within yourself to find that person who would strike out at an ex with vindictive vengeance. Maybe revenge isn't your style. And that's cool. As much as these pages focus on revenge, in the end, revenge is something that might end up being the last resort for you. You may decide that revenge can sometimes taste sweet, but pride tastes better. Bottom line: Providing for your own happiness is the only true way you'll get revenge. Whatever you do to reach that point, even if it's just living vicariously through all the remarkable tales in this book, is entirely your call. Make sure that the path you choose is the one that will most satisfy you . . . and keep you out of jail.

Breakups, divorces, and surprise bisexual orgies can be a hair-raising and hair-pulling time in one's life. They provide an interesting fork in the road of life. Which way will you go? Sometimes it's best to move on. Sometimes it's worth pausing and contemplating your options. But sometimes, deciding to serve up an ice-cold dish of revenge is the special of the day.

You just have to decide if you have the appetite for it.

Chapter 1

READYING FOR WAR

If you prick us, do we not bleed? If you tickle us, do we not laugh? If you poison us, do we not die? And if you wrong us, shall we not revenge?—William Shakespeare, *The Merchant of Venice*

You think you're being cheated on but your man isn't fessing up to anything. Or you think your man is strategizing how to kick you to the curb. Or maybe you've just had the ugly truth thrown in your face out of the clear blue: You've been cheated on and then dumped. Or maybe you've been cheated on, dumped, and left with a nasty and volatile STD. And now that unbearable sensation (I'm talking about the heartache, not the clap) won't go away. Maybe he told you it was over or maybe you told him he wasn't going to cheat on you again because you were kicking him out. Whatever the reason, solution, or end result, being dumped or cheated on bites the proverbial big one. Anyone knows that without having to actually go through it. So how do you make sure to prepare yourself in case that's about to happen to you?

Let's rewind. Were you suspicious but didn't really focus on obvious signs for fear of discovering the truth? Or did this all come out of left field because you were so gaga over the bastard and just blindly trusted him? If you could back up in time and acknowledge—and act on—your suspicions, you probably would have found yourself at the filing cabinet going through past credit-card charges or sifting through receipts like a madwoman because, well, you would have been a madwoman. This would have been the closest you would have come to a straitjacket, but for good reason. You would have had to make sure you were right. You would have had to put two and two together accurately before super-gluing his butt cheeks together.

So, are you now able to see the handwriting on the very wall you're banging your head against? Are you wondering why you didn't notice the neon signs he was shining while he was screwing your yoga class friend in the lotus position? And, looking back on it now, why in the hell was he going to swim at the YMCA wearing Drakkar Noir?

> **If you marry a man who cheats on his wife, you'll be married to a man who cheats on his wife.—Ann Landers**

Even the brightest of us don't always see what's going on right under our noses. It's because of one glaring and gratuitously egotistical reason: We don't want to. Our egos are so much more sensitive and delicate than our hearts. The thought of rejection, the fear of being alone, and the anxiety of having to get "out there" again and date are just too much to handle. You make "sensitivity concessions" with yourself for his sake and yours. You've already invested so many of these concessions in the relationship: You made peace with his farting, his smelly sock-balls, and his sexual insecurities long ago.

But most of our sensitivity concessions are fragile. Unlike the dead French president François Mitterrand's wife, we have to apply a "handle with care" label when it comes to our own feelings. When President Mitterrand died, his wife attended the funeral stoically. Also in attendance were the dead president's mistress and illegitimate daughter. Talk about leaving this world a "bitter" place. *Zut alors!*

There were three of us in this marriage, so it was a bit crowded.—Diana, Princess of Wales, on Prince Charles and Camilla Parker Bowles, in a BBC1 *Panorama* interview

The Cheat Is On

This chapter will shed some light on cheating because both those men who are about to dump you and those men who are cheating on you frequently exhibit similar behavior. Of course, the cheater often wants you back. The affair is usually a sideshow event that he knows should come to an end, and when it does, he may even feel a euphoric sensation that highlights his feelings for you and may cause him to be overly erotic or lovey-dovey around you in the immediate aftermath.

Love is a game in which one always cheats.—Honoré de Balzac

He may, of course, also try to blame it on the fact that studies have come out that it's just part of his genetic makeup. A 2008 study by Swedish researchers at the Karolinska Institute found that there's a gene, AVPR1A, which literally messes with a guy's head—it affects a brain chemical. It's a gene that's very similar in humans and voles, and explains why certain types of voles are monogamous, and why others aren't. Ditto for human men. If they have the gene (and supposedly 40 percent of men do), chances are they'll end up cheating, or at least unable to commit. That's one helluva excuse—imagine how many guys are running around to find some doctors to help them prove they've got just that!

In the long run, if he's cheating on you, for whatever reason, things will either come to a sledgehammer of an ending or are going to be super crappy between you two for a long time. But if you're willing to try to rectify things in order to salvage your relationship—which many people do, whether because they have kids together, a house together, or simply feelings they can't erase—it's not something you can always fix with Dr. Phil, couple's pornography, or home cooking. Especially when you realize that when boys start playing in another backyard, they come home only wanting to see more of the neighborhood.

Maybe he'll realize his mistake and not make the same one twice. Perhaps that's wishful thinking; perhaps it's possible. But in this book, we're not giving him the benefit of the doubt. We're going with the more realistic notion that he needs a little reminding of what it means to mess with you.

The Lying, Stinking, Cheating Populace

Thinking Ahead

Catherine Zeta-Jones is rumored to have an infidelity clause in her prenup with Michael Douglas stating that he has to pay her millions if he ever cheats.

The numbers on who is cheating are all over the place: some, many, fewer than expected, off the charts. These huge disparities may be due to people's highly flexible definitions of "cheating" (is a blow job considered a sexual infraction?) or to the fact that many people don't provide honest answers when asked about their sex lives. It's not like an exit poll on Election Day. Some people just may not be ready to relinquish that information, no matter how confidential the questionnaire. As one *New York Times* article, "Love, Sex and the Changing Landscape of Infidelity," suggests, "Surveys conducted in person are likely to underestimate the real rate of adultery, because people are reluctant to admit such behavior not just to their spouses but to anyone." So the facts on adultery have never been completely clear.

When cheated, wife or husband feels the same.—Euripides

Before 1988, national statistics were limited to fertility-related behavior and to sexual behavior in adolescence. According to Tom W. Smith, director of the General Social Survey and director of the Center for the Study of Politics and Society at the National Opinion Research Center (NORC), "It really was only the advent of AIDS and the heightened public policy need to have good solid statistics on adult sexual behavior that led to the increased data collection on that topic." Don't blame the National Security Administration, but scientists have been able to do a bit more sex research than they could before and gain access to more truthful answers.

I did not have sexual relations with that woman, Miss Lewinsky.—President Bill Clinton

Whatever the numbers, one thing is clear: People cheat. But according to the March 2006 NORC survey, "American

Sexual Behavior," the "facts" on extramarital affairs are more hotly disputed than the findings on any other area of human behavior. This is the result of pop-psychology experts and magazines, which conduct their own "studies" on sexual behavior in the United States. "These studies typically find an extremely high level of extramarital activity. They also often claim that extramarital relations have become much more common over time. In actual fact, the data indicates much more stability than change," says Smith. "Three to four percent of currently married people have a sexual partner besides their spouse in a given year, and fifteen to eighteen percent of ever-married people have had a sexual partner other than their spouse while married" (according to a 1994 journal article by Robert T. Michael, Edward O. Laumann, and John H. Gagnon). That means that if you're in a room with ten people, one of them has put his hose in the wrong garden and another person is probably planting a seed.

I have good-looking kids. Thank goodness my wife cheats on me.—Rodney Dangerfield

However, one thing does appear to have changed: As Smith states, "There is some indication of a narrowing of the gap between men and women on the level of extramarital relationship." With more women getting out of the house to go to work, and sexual taboos becoming a thing of the past (with the help of TV shows such as *Sex and the City* and *Desperate Housewives*), women are feeling more entitled to a little bit of their own fun. Or maybe they've always cheated just as much but were better at lying about it. According to private investigator

Vinny Parco, owner of Intercontinental Investigations and star of the Court TV show *Parco PI*, another reason women cheat is "they're bored." As Parco explains: "Their husbands are not noticing them anymore or taking care of them. Or they caught their husband years ago cheating and now it's their turn. It's revenge." Touché.

However, there have been studies that have shown at least women are much better at sensing potential "threats" (hot guys other than their mates) and have the ability to recognize when they should make the effort to protect their relationships. Researchers at McGill University in Montreal developed a study that revealed that women literally had alarms going off in their heads if they found themselves flirting (which could lead to cheating), while men, on the other hand, barely seemed to notice that they might be flirting with disaster. The conclusion was made that men need some training so that they learn how to avoid finding themselves surrounded by a bevy of beauties while out with friends, all while their significant other is doing their laundry and waiting for them to come home.

> Mr. Zhang Bin is having an illicit relationship with a woman other than me.—Hu Ziwei, wife of Zhang Bin, a popular Chinese TV sportscaster. Hu Ziwei busted into the Beijing Olympics press conference, making her announcement for the whole world to hear.

MSNBC.com and iVillage conducted a survey in February 2007, getting responses from more than 70,000 readers during a two-week period. "Three-quarters told us they were in a committed relationship and the majority of participants have been with their current partner for at least 12 years. Fifty-four percent were men, with an average age of 43; 46 percent were women, 38 was their average age."

According to their study, nearly half of the men and women surveyed had cheated. "Twenty-two percent of people have cheated on their current partner, but only 4 percent are in the middle of an affair."

Flowers Are a Wife's Divorce Attorney's Best Friend

Leroy Greer from Texas sued 1-800-Flowers, claiming a "breach of contract" because he had specifically asked that no documentation be sent to his home when he ordered flowers for his mistress. But months later, the Internet flower delivery business sent him a thank-you note, and his wife—from whom he was separated at the time—found it. Although the couple was already in the middle of a divorce, this episode definitely punctuated their marriage and hit his wallet—she's asking for a hell of a lot more money now with the proof of infidelity on her side.

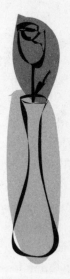

According to the Ashley Madison Agency (www.ashley madison.com), a Web site that *promotes* infidelity and has slogans that include "When Monogamy Becomes Monotony" and "Life Is Short, Have an Affair," "50 to 60 percent of men and 40 to 50 percent of women will engage in an extramarital affair or romantic tryst at some point." They also point out that 50 percent of Americans said, "President Clinton's adultery makes his moral standard about the same as [that of] the average married man."

So, if you go by those numbers, when you walk past five people—male or female—on any given day, you can take it to the bank that at least two of them have been "sexually barnstorming."

Miller's Double-Crossing

Everyone and their mother knows Jude Law cheated on his former fiancée actress Sienna Miller with his children's nanny. But after calling off the engagement, Miller found a way to forgive Law, patch things up, and then apparently get back at him—by "hanging out" with the latest 007, Daniel Craig. Law and Miller then went kaput.

The Politicians

As an illustration of how cheating happens in every walk of life, let's check out a high-profile arena, in which one would assume that cheating would be curbed due to the elevated risk of getting caught: politics. When a lawmaker gets busted with his pants (or her skirt) wrapped around his ankles, it's splashed on the front pages. You'd think that'd be incentive enough to stop any sort of office sex play, right? Wrong.

Here are just a few examples of politicians recently in the spotlight for pork-barreling women—and men—who aren't their wives:

While campaigning for the presidency, preaching moral values and putting his devotion to his cancer-stricken wife on display, former Democratic presidential candidate John Edwards got busted for having an affair with a filmmaker who was documenting his campaign. (Despite Edwards's denials, rumors also swirled that he had fathered her child.)

Former New Jersey governor Jim McGreevey came out of the closet and admitted he had cheated on his wife with another man. Later on, he claimed that she participated in threesomes with him and his lover, but she denied it.

Client Number 9 (aka former governor of New York Eliot Spitzer) dipped his icicle into a $1,000-an-hour call girl's Sno-Cone while he was busting prostitution rings and proving to be a hard-liner on crime. He was hard, all right.

Reverend Ted Haggard, former president of the National Evangelical Association, regularly condemned homosexuality. But then he was accused of having sex with another man— who also happened to be his meth dealer.

How about U.S. Senator Larry Craig, who was caught red-*footed* playing footsie in a bathroom stall with a man who turned out to be an undercover police officer.

While former House Speaker Newt Gingrich was blasting President Clinton for playing around with Monica Lewinsky, he was cheating on his wife as well. You have to understand: Infidelity is very bipartisan.

Which of course brings us to the godfather of infidelity, former president Bill Clinton, who was doing more than actually smoking the presidential cigars in his chambers with Monica.

> CNN found that Hillary Clinton is the most admired woman in America. Women admire her because she's strong and successful. Men admire her because she allows her husband to cheat and get away with it.—Jay Leno

The Thinkers

> Believe me, to seek a quarrel with a man is a bad method of pleasing the woman who loves that man.—Alexandre Dumas, *The Count of Monte Cristo*

To move away from politics and turn toward a more philosophical approach to the concept of cheating, there are those who, like the French novelist Marcel Proust, believe that the threat of infidelity isn't necessarily a bad thing, but rather the secret to a long-lasting relationship. "Adultery introduces spirit into what otherwise might have been the dead letter of marriage," Proust poetically mused. "A woman one loves rarely suffices for all our needs, so we deceive her with another whom we do not love."

And while you may want to jump to the conclusion that all men are egomaniacal pigs, some women follow that same pattern of thought. Anthropologist Margaret Mead suggested that monogamy is an extremely tricky practice. "Monogamous heterosexual love is probably one of the most difficult, complex, and demanding of human relationships," she said—even when it came to her own life (she was married three times). "I do feel I've given monogamy—in an absolute sense—a pretty fair trial—and found it wanting."

Parrotting Love

One parrot made things a little complicated for Suzy Collins when he began squawking, "I love you, Gary" and "Hi Gary" whenever her phone would ring—all in front of her boyfriend (and the parrot's owner), Chris Taylor. Turns out, Suzy had been having an affair with her ex-colleague Gary, and had had him over numerous times in the apartment she shared with Chris. When things fluttered to light, the girlfriend moved out, and soon enough, Chris also had to get rid of his bird since it wouldn't stop calling out Gary's name.

There are those who find monogamy to be flat-out boring, more a recognition of some fundamental failure of the imagination than a virtue. Oscar Wilde chimed, "Those who are faithful know only the trivial side of love: it is the faithless who know love's tragedies." Leo Tolstoy's *Anna Karenina*, Gustave Flaubert's *Madame Bovary*, and Nathaniel Hawthorne's *The Scarlet Letter* are among our great works of literature. Perhaps it's no accident that their protagonists are all caught up in tempestuous, catastrophic, adulterous affairs.

That's the common thread in all their stories, and it seems to pertain to everyday life as well. Why can't we remain in marital bliss and not have to suffer? Is there really no escape from experiencing the trials and tribulations of a love that strays? Why is it so rare to find the "happily married after" with no bumps, potholes, or near-fatal relationship accidents such as infidelity along the road?

The woman who is adulterous in her own home must always remember one thing—put the seat down.—William Cole

Writer Claire Booth Luce once said, "There's nothing like a good dose of another woman to make a man appreciate his wife." But this is just a dispassionate theory on adultery. A writer's philosophy is probably the furthest thing from your mind when you find out your husband has been poking someone else's pie.

Husbands are chiefly good as lovers when they are betraying their wives.—Marilyn Monroe

So what happens once the red-lettered elephant called infidelity is in the room? According to iVillage and MSNBC.com, 13 percent of women and 18 percent of men decided to forget about it and stayed together. Forty-four percent of women and 37 percent of men couldn't get over it and left their partner. Eleven percent of the women who cheated said it was to get even with the spouse for something he did, while only 5 percent of men could say it was for revenge.

Is Monogamy Natural?

In *The Myth of Monogamy: Fidelity and Infidelity in Animals and People,* David Barash and Judith Lipton remind us that monogamy is rare in animals. The only monogamous primates? The marmoset and tamarin monkeys.

Whatever the percentages are, it's time to get the down and dirty facts on what's going on in your "other half's" life when he's not around you. You don't need an eyepiece, a pipe, and a trench coat to figure it out, but you may have to tap into the sleuth region of your brain in order to discover the truth.

Chapter 2

WARNING SHOTS!

So how do you really know if your spouse or lover is whoring around the world? Will you ever know? Is the household routine feeling out of whack? What about things between the sheets? Are they still red hot or are they soggy cold? Is this a sign that your husband has moved onto "greener ass-tures"? (Okay, that was bad.)

> I've looked on a lot of women with lust. I've committed adultery in my heart many times. This is something that God recognizes I will do—and I have done it—and God forgives me for it.—then-governor Jimmy Carter in an interview with *Playboy* magazine

Let's look for some basic signs, patterns, and future incriminating evidence. Various research has found that there is always a trail (or technically, "slime") that cheating husbands leave behind.

Is Your Phone on Vibrate?

There's the alleged story of the man who kept calling his girlfriend, who he suspected was cheating on him. Her phone would ring and ring, but she wouldn't answer. Finally, he decided to surprise her by walking in on her, thinking he was about to catch her with another man; instead, it turned out she was masturbating to the ringing phone whenever it was him calling.

When searching for evidence of dark behavior, you need to remember that you can jump to hasty conclusions that can trigger your rage and, before you know it, rash actions you may regret. Just because your lover exhibits one or two of the behaviors listed doesn't mean he's definitely cheating. Don't go pissing in his coffee just because you find breath mints in his pants.

For example, let's say after you saw all of your husband's autographed baseball bats in half, you get a phone call from him in which he says he'll explain everything. He convinces you to meet him at your local dive bar. You do so reluctantly, not even bothering to change out of your sweats and chocolate-stained T-shirt. You're ready for him to be on his knees, begging for your forgiveness, desperately wanting to get you back. You show up and are surprised—literally. Everyone's there, all of your closest friends and family, and he's the one who organized it: a huge surprise party to celebrate your promotion at work.

Or you come home early to find the front door slightly ajar; there's music on, a tune you two never listen to, and rose petals are leading the way into the kitchen. You tiptoe down the hall, grab a camera, and throw open the kitchen door, shooting off a photo in order to have concrete evidence of him in the "act." In-stead, you only scare the hell out of your hubby, who is sweating profusely while attempting to cook your favorite meal, making him drop the food on the floor. He wanted to cook for you, to surprise you for no particular reason except to remind you that he loves you.

You screwed up and jumped the gun. Your vengeful mind was misguided. And now you may have caused your relationship to be on the fritz for no good reason. So be careful what you do and how you conduct your research, Sherlock, until you really know what's going on with your lover or spouse. At the same time, if a guy cheats, the longer he doesn't get caught, the more he thinks he can get away with it without hurting anyone. So let the pieces of the puzzle fall into place because it will all come out in the wash, especially if he's doing multiple loads.

> I think a man can have two, maybe three affairs while he is married. But three is the absolute maximum. After that, you are cheating.—Yves Montand

Some signs to look for (not necessarily in this order):

- He's suddenly got all this stuff to do outside of the home (e.g., working late, going to change the car's oil at 10:30 P.M., taking business trips to Daytona Beach).
- He's not that into sex anymore (he says he has a headache, rushes to be asleep before you, or simply rejects physical advances).
- When he *is* having sex with you, he's switching behavior, or positions (covering your face with the sheets, asking to try the "wheelbarrow" position or the "Bulbous Big Butthole Breach").
- He's picking stupid fights (by telling you that your clothes-folding skills are subpar, that your cooking

could use help, that those pants are looking tight on you).

- He's suddenly buying you gifts and doing good deeds (e.g., French toast in the morning, doing way too much laundry, letting you watch *Grey's Anatomy* during the World Series).
- He's spaced out (you wake up in the morning to find him staring at the ceiling; you find him sitting in his car in the driveway, staring at the wheel; or you find him in the kitchen, staring at the toast he just charred).
- He's impossible to connect with at work (his secretary says, "Sorry, Mr. Smith stepped out for another slice of pizza," "Sorry, Mr. Franklin's in another meeting," "Sorry, Mr. Hughes got the wrong type of Post-its again and went to return them at Staples himself").
- He's become more secretive. (Remember those funny passwords you came up with for each other's e-mail accounts? His isn't working anymore.)
- He's working on his image, finally (using lotion, suddenly conscious about designer clothes, using cologne you bought him five years ago).

I do not think that there are any men who are faithful to their wives.—Jacqueline Kennedy Onassis

The list goes on and on:

- When he hugs you, he pats you on the back as if you're softball teammates.
- He's lost interest in discussing any future plans like home remodeling, vacations, or meeting your grandmother.

- He's not calling you back right away and/or he's screening your calls.
- He's discreetly switching off his phone and pager when he's with you.
- He's whining about being unappreciated, even after you offer oral sex.
- You get in the car and realize that the passenger seat is not in the usual position.
- He's only using the computer when he's alone.
- His Web browser history contains MySpace, Facebook, or other social gathering sites that he never visited before.
- You find a different e-mail account open on a Web mail site.
- He's become much more interested in your weekly schedule.
- He runs out for milk and comes back an hour later, blaming the extended five-minute drive on traffic or lines or running into an old friend.
- He can't remember certain payments on the bank statements, but says he'll pay them anyway.
- He starts carrying lots of cash in his wallet.
- His wallet's also stuffed with unexplained receipts.
- He's carrying around phone cards.
- He's accusing *you* of having an affair to try to throw you off his track and make you question your state of mind!

Parental Guidance

In his book *The Dangerous Passion: Why Jealousy Is as Necessary as Love and Sex*, author David Buss recounts an urban legend about a man named "Mike" who comes home to tell his dad he's found the woman he's going to marry. When his dad hears who the lucky lady is, he confides in his son that he didn't have the most exciting sex life with his son's mother, and he fooled around a lot. And this girl actually happens to be Mike's half sister.

Mike is upset but soon enough gets over it and finds someone else. When he comes home to announce his impending marriage, his father again explains that this girl is also his half sister, due to his father's indiscretions.

Furious, Mike goes to his mother and tells her everything, adding that at this rate, he'll never marry. But the mother simply shakes her head and tells him, "Don't worry; he's not really your father."

The following signs should be taken very seriously. If he's exhibiting them, he's either cheating on you, delirious, or planning a surprise party (let's hope there's something to celebrate!):

- He ducks into other rooms or leaves the house to talk on the phone.
- You get hang-ups on your home phone.
- Strange women, whom he calls business colleagues, leave suspicious messages on your voice mail.
- His cell phone has unfamiliar numbers stored or dialed.

- His clothes are laced with makeup or lipstick smudges.
- His clothes smell of perfume, massage oil residue, and good old-fashioned *Eau de Fucking*.
- He does his own laundry (you might as well let this behavior ride as long as possible before confronting him).
- He doesn't come home till the morning hours, saying he had to pull an all-nighter at work.
- He's off on another business trip.

Divorce: The Gift That Keeps on Giving

Getting money from your ex—and also reminding him that you had something to do with his financial success—is always a nice, dirty way to get revenge and stick it where it often hurts most: the wallet. (Remember what Ivana Trump said after she and the Donald split ways? "Don't get mad—get everything!") According to *Forbes* magazine, here are what some male icons had to pay to their exes.

Top Ten Celebrity Divorces

1. Basketball superstar Michael Jordan: $150 million plus. He shoots, she scores!
2. Singer Neil Diamond: $150 million. "Girl, You'll Be a Rich Woman Soon."

3. Film director Steven Spielberg: $100 million. *Raiders of the Lost Divorce Proceedings.*

4. Actor Harrison Ford: $85 million. *The Temple of Prenuptials.* (His ex, Melissa Mathison, also smartly negotiated a piece of Ford's *future* earnings from films he made while married, such as royalties from DVD and video sales of the *Indiana Jones* trilogy.)

5. Actor Kevin Costner: $80 million. *Settles with Wolves.*

6. Beatle Sir Paul McCartney: Possibly $60 million. "Love Me Don't."

7. Film director James Cameron: $50 million. *Judgment Day: Terminated.*

8. Actor Michael Douglas: $45 million. *Romancing the Bones.*

9. Singer Lionel Richie: $20 million. "Pay You, Say Me."

10. Singer Mick Jagger: $15 to $25 million. "Jumpin' Jack Cash."

And since this list was put together, we should add the messy divorces of Charlie Sheen and Denise Richards *(It's Complicated)*, Kim Basinger and Alec Baldwin (who called his daughter a "thoughtless little pig"), and Ellen Barkin and Ron Perelman (Barkin sued the billionaire for the measly $3.4 million that he had promised her production company).

Blowing Up Divorce

Doctor Nicholas Bartha was quite determined that his ex-wife get absolutely nothing from their divorce, so he blew up his multi-million-dollar Manhattan townhouse in an apparent suicide attempt, sending the message to his estranged wife "If I can't have it, neither can you." Somewhere in there, I suspect, he still lost more than she did.

Golden Parachutes Gone Wrong

In 2002, Jane Welch, former wife of General Motors CEO Jack Welch, wasn't satisfied with the amount she was to get in her divorce settlement when it was revealed that Jack was having an affair with another woman. So she clued the media in on what Jack was getting as part of his retirement package, like a $80,000-a-month Manhattan condo. It wasn't a good time for CEOs to be loaded with such benefits (is it ever?), so Jack had to drop a lot of these perks in order to save face—and his name. Although the final divorce settlement was done in private, it's thought that she managed to embarrass him into giving her a lot more cash.

And Sometimes It's All Worth It . . .

Iris Rodriguez divorced her husband, Juan, just days before he won the $149 million jackpot in 2004 in the Mega Millions lottery. Good timing!

Where the Truth Lies

So, are you ready to confront him? Of course, most men will deny an affair—unless there's absolutely no denying it (for example, you catch him butt naked, slapping someone else's naked ass with his hands and other . . . uh . . . appendages). But what can you look out for without having to strap a lie detector on him? Have a security expert interrogate him? Or bring him on an embarrassing reality TV show that supposedly separates fact from fiction in front of millions of viewers?

Amazing what kind of language the body speaks without using the tongue, and how much you can hear if you're really watching. Here are some telltale signs that he's lying when you ask him about his possible extracurricular activities (remember, these are considered "signs" if they represent unusual behavior for him):

Face: Is he nodding while saying "no"? Can he not keep a straight face? Does he look you directly in the eyes but have a smirk? Or does he keep laughing, blaming it on a memory of a funny time between the two of you and trying to switch the subject to that?

Nose: Does he suddenly have allergies? Is he blowing his nose obsessively, even though he doesn't have a cold? Or is he just rubbing it, as if he's suddenly developed a coke habit?

Ears: Do the tips of his ears redden when you broach the subject of "white stains" on his Dockers?

Eyes: Those eyes you once gazed into lovingly, are they now looking back at you but darting every which way when he utters, "No, I'm not sleeping with someone else"? There's a saying: It's all in the eyes . . . or is it?

Mouth: How many times have you kissed those lips? Now is he covering those lips when he speaks?

Body: That body that you were so attracted to, that you've seen naked so many times, that's been wrapped around you in so many different positions—does it now seem like a different body? Is your man tense, standoff-ish, squirmy, even twitching? Is he sweating like a steel-worker? Is he shaking like a heroin addict? Is he clearing his throat like a magistrate? Pretty obvious, but stuff you may overlook when you are in a different state of mind. Is he turning away from you completely so all you see is his back? (Does he suddenly notice the cracks in the living room ceiling? Has he decided to dig through his closet to chuck those clothes you've wanted him to get rid of for so long now? Has he suddenly become a handyman and climbed under the kitchen sink to fix that leak you've been complaining about?) Does he look uncomfortable? If he looks uncomfortable, your questions are probably making him exactly that!

Arms: Is he hugging himself? Wrapping a "protective shield" around himself?

Hands: Are they glued inside his pockets? Or is he making big gestures, like he's suddenly giving a political speech? Or does he suddenly have a rash? Is he scratching his head, his cheek, his ear, his nose, his arm, his leg? Is he suddenly cracking all of his knuckles in every way possible?

Legs: Could he be the perfect spokesman for someone with restless legs syndrome?

Feet: Is he shifting his feet, unable to stand still?

Behavior: When you sit down to chat, does he put things between you two? Like, move the ottoman in front of himself or place a full cup of coffee so that there's no reaching over without spilling it? Or does he start surfing the Web, with his laptop on his lap, the back of it like a plastic wall? Or does he start doing things he normally doesn't do—like brush his teeth midafternoon, right when you've started on the subject, or iron a shirt (something he never does!) he will need for a meeting two days from now? When you suddenly change the subject from this touchy one, is he suddenly more relaxed and at ease, thinking you've forgotten it?

Speech: What happens when he opens his mouth to speak? Is he not answering you directly? Rather, is he making a general statement so that there's room for him to avoid stating the exact truth? Or is he talking super fast, a mile a minute, on various topics to avoid the subject at hand? Is he changing the subject, running out because he's late, or talking over you, saying he knows what you're going to say and that it's crazy?

All these different signs can help, but truth be told, you will only be able to know if he's lying (without hard evidence and proof) by your own sixth sense. Go with your instinct, your gut, and as much rationale as possible. Hopefully, you'll be able to figure out the difference between fact and fiction.

The Passenger Seat

So, you're fairly certain you're involved with a cheater or someone who's about to dump you. You've broached the subject and all you got were unusual signs coming from him, as if he's lying. No confession was made, but now the handwriting's all over the wall and you're going through one of the worst stages: the uncertainty. You're hoping that you've got it all wrong somehow. That you've misread the signs. That you're just a crazy, controlling, jealous bitch who completely misunderstands her husband's behavior and completely underappreciates who he is.

Airing Out Down and Dirty Laundry

The reality TV show *Cheaters* was created so that people could confront their cheating lovers on national television. And it was a voyeuristic way to peep into other people's lives.

The show's investigative team spied on the suspect and then showed the evidence to the victim. Things usually got a little hairy on the show when the victim confronted his or her cheating partner when he or she was getting it on at some

---

seedy motel—and this was all caught on camera. The show took a turn for the worse when the host, Joey Greco, was stabbed while boarding a fishing boat with a woman to confront her husband and his mistress. While the event was called an accident, this was scary nonetheless.

But are you irrationally jumping the gun? How will you know for sure? You have to find out before you grill him with a spotlight and waft cigarette smoke through venetian blinds. You don't want to accuse him without evidence—if you're wrong, it could put a serious dent in that thing called "trust."

And if it's all horribly true, be prepared, because hearing the truth straight from the horse's mouth may be more devastating than you think, no matter how thoroughly you've anticipated the worst. Be mentally prepared and calm when you present him with the evidence. Think through every word, everything you say, no matter how odd the pause in conversation feels. You must remain in control. Men usually expect women to be erratic during these types of confrontations. So when you show him a calm and collected self, he'll be flustered and caught off guard by your rationality and tact.

Putting the Marriage in Reverse

Clara Harris drove over her husband *several* times when she found out he was banging his secretary in the same hotel they were married in.

A 2003 survey by Symantec, a U.S. antivirus and Internet security firm, suggested that if women suspected cheating, 40 percent of them would snoop in a partner's e-mail account, compared with only 25 percent of men who would do so. When it came to text messages, 62 percent of women said they'd check their partner's phones, but only 39 percent of men said they'd bother.

So what would you do to find out the truth? According to the previously cited MSNBC.com and iVillage survey, "87 percent of men and women would try to trick their partner into confessing, but only 20 percent of them would directly confront their partner with suspicions. More than half would be willing to snoop on e-mail, and the majority of respondents would check phone logs or phone bills."

It's like the National Security Agency out there. Here are some ways to join the club.

It depends on what the meaning of the word *is* is.— President Bill Clinton, during his 1998 grand jury testimony on the Monica Lewinsky affair

Red-Handed Bandit

You need to find out if he's cheating, but at this point, drastic action is needed. The following possibilities might give

 you some ideas on how to catch him, making it a cinch or a pinch. But watch yourself: Some of these deceptions may have you looking in the mirror and asking yourself, "Has it really come to this?" Always remember that usually the easiest and most problem-free way to deal with a spouse you're suspicious of is to confront him honestly. Depending on how the confrontation goes, you can then decide on your future with or without him.

But you bought this book for the juicy details that accompany revenge. So let's see how to trap the rat.

Set him up in a bar or a place he frequents often and have an anonymous friend act as bait. See if he hits on her—and hopefully, she'll report back! God have mercy on him if he uses a pickup line that he used on you (oh, and ideally, she should be wired so she can record him as well, just in case he needs his memory jolted).

Pretend you're going out of town but check into a local hotel or stay at a friend's place, then watch the house from a distance. You'll find out a lot, and it's kind of intriguing to feel as if you're on a stakeout. But those long, endless hours in the car can put you to sleep, so make sure not to miss all the action when something finally does happen!

If you've got the fallopians to follow him, track him down, stay out of sight, and find out if he is really going to meet his mistress. Seeing is believing.

Press redial or *69 on his phone. Find out who he's been calling—or who's been calling him. Just as e-mail has replaced letter writing, cell phones and their caller IDs are making the art of cheating—and the art of detection—easier.

Check the first outgoing cell-phone call of the day and the last call at night, and see if the calls are to the same number. Most cheaters call their lovers as soon as they wake up and just before they go to bed. Note the time of incoming calls, especially those of hang-ups. And of course, check his cell-phone bill, since it is usually itemized with the numbers of all incoming and outgoing calls.

Note the mileage on his car before and after trips or evenings out, and see if something looks unusual (like he drove an extra fifty miles on a workday when he said he didn't even take lunch). And take advantage of those E-ZPass tollbooth statements (if you live in places like New York), which can reveal which tunnels and bridges he really was zipping through or over and when.

Become unpredictable. If you're always punctual, start showing up a good twenty minutes late. Or call to say that you're going to be late and then show up early. See if he notices at all. If he starts questioning you about your sudden schedule change, trying to figure out if this is going to continue, you may be right to suspect. Or if you catch him at home just dusting his sports memorabilia and being uncharacteristically nonchalant that you suddenly showed up unexpectedly, he could be secretly thanking his gods that he wasn't cheating that day.

Are you on Facebook? There's an application that reveals an electronic map of someone's location through his or her cell phone. Called the Social Network Integrated Friend Finder (Sniff), it can locate anyone, anytime, anywhere—but the person "sniffed" out has to approve of being located, whether by specific people or by everyone. This racks up a few more dollars on your cell-phone bill. The bonus: If you get lost, you can "sniff" yourself out and to the right location. The downside: got an employer paying your phone bill? They may decide to sniff you out during your lunch when you're chowing down on something other than a turkey BLT. Obviously, this can work wonders for women who want to know where their husbands have been.

Now everyone can be a CIA agent. Some cell phones can be secretly placed under a car seat or left in a bedroom. When they are phoned from anywhere, they don't make any noise but are activated as listening devices. One program, FlexiSpy, dubbed "Trojan horse spy" or just "Trojan," installs secretly on cell phones to monitor calls and text messages. And now Flexi-Spy Pro offers call history, e-mail recording, and location tracking features, plus remote monitoring and Subscriber Identity Module change information. That means you can basically listen in real time to what the cell-phone owner is doing anywhere!

Buy software that will serve as your eyes and ears on his computer. You can find out if he's having an online affair or is addicted to Internet porn. I don't know which one's worse: Topeka Singles Chat or Jenna Jameson.

Advanced spyware programs are available to help you find out about any cyber relationships. Spector, developed by Spectorsoft, acts like a fast-clicking camera, taking photos every few seconds of whatever shows up on-screen. The pictures are then played back as if in a slide show. There are even key-logging software programs that record every key typed. So no matter how daunting hacking into a computer may seem, the process is now dumbed-down for even the most amateur of us slighted geeks.

If you suspect he's using dating Web sites, set up a fake profile online of what you know he likes in a woman—and see if he bites! It's a long shot, but if he does . . . awkward!

There are also Web sites devoted to doing things like tracing any personal information you may need. One is I.C.U. Inc. (www.tracerservices.com), which does asset searches, background checks, bug sweeps, cheating spouses investigations, etc. FYI-SPY (www.fyi-spy.com) monitors all keystrokes, sites visited, and conversations that happen on the computer, and it's private. Well, not for him anymore.

Infidelitytoday.com offers a DNA testing kit. It's a kit that can detect semen on men's underwear after sex. Helpful to know, especially if the two of you are no longer having sex!

Spy Web sites are great places to outfit your devious plot. FollowThatCar.com boasts a GPS Vehicle Tracking System. Slip a GPS into his car to monitor his whereabouts. You can find out his exact location from a remote area. The GPS can be peeled off the car each night and attached to your computer, where it will reveal a map of that day's journey.

SpyZone.com and The Spy Store, Inc. (www.thespystore.com), have everything from night-vision goggles to video and audio surveillance devices to detection scramblers to bulletproof products to voice stress analysis machines to police badges. If you don't catch him cheating, at least you'll have the equipment to be able to operate undercover in Pakistan.

That's an initial list. A reminder: Nothing beats the good old-fashioned method of sitting him down and asking him face-to-face if he's cheating. But acting like a sleuth can be fun—if you can learn to enjoy discovering the down and dirty truth about your relationship.

Working at Breaking Up

Can't face your coworkers or your job after a nasty breakup? One Japanese marketing company, Hime & Company, allows for a "heartache leave" to those who have just broken up, giving them a little time to cry and get over their lost love. The company is also respectful of age and of how much harder it is to get over someone/find someone new the older you get: Under twenty-four, you get one day off if you broke up with someone; between twenty-five and twenty-nine, you get two days off, and after thirty, you have three days to gain weight from ice cream and watch reruns of *Benji*.

The Good Dicks

The fictitious "That Girl Emily" from the Court TV/Deep Focus advertising campaign started to see the signs that "Steven" was cheating on her: taking his phone calls in the other room,

staying late at work, not being interested in the bedroom. In order to confirm her suspicions (and of course to tie in what was being advertised), Emily (or rather, her brother) hired a private investigator to follow her husband and get footage on what he was doing and who he was with. Nothing shouts the truth louder and clearer than concrete photographs and video. Especially when you get them hand-delivered by the guy you paid big bucks to get them: a private investigator.

The first thing that might come to mind when you hear "private investigator" is the cold, dark days of cynical private dicks, lipsticked damsels, or bad guys settling scores with ice picks. Or maybe it's gumshoes strolling the streets in trench coats and fedoras, and never using an umbrella when it rains. But PIs specializing in finding out about your lover's extracurricular activities are on the rise worldwide. What exactly do they do? Are they effective? Do they carry guns? Do they all talk with a funny accent? Are venetian blinds in all of their offices? How much is this film noir setting going to cost you?

Some PIs charge an hourly rate for surveillance; some will do it for a flat fee with mileage and expenses added later. But does that really matter to you? Your blood is boiling and you want answers. Just don't shit a kitten when you see the credit-card bill. Prepare yourself, because using a private investigator can add up quick.

Friendly Investigations

"Tara's" friend "Susan" had a boyfriend, "Ted," who cheated on her repeatedly. Every time Susan caught wind of this, Ted would beg her to not break up with him, saying he'd never do it again. She would go back to him every time, even though Tara told her once a cheater, always a cheater. But Susan was optimistic.

Susan and Tara were chatting on the phone one evening, and Susan seemed stressed. She said something was up again with Ted but she wasn't sure what exactly. So Tara decided that instant to put an end to it all. She asked Susan where he was, and Susan told her he was at a bar with a group of his friends. Tara wrote down the name of the bar, despite Susan's having told her she was sure everything was fine and that Ted would be coming back to her later.

Tara got dressed up and put on a wig. She also put on a hat and a fake British accent, and grabbed a friend, who got dolled up, too. They found the bar where Ted was with his guy friends. Ted didn't recognize Tara, even though they had met before. Tara and her friends started to flirt with the group and they all started to party together. After three hours of jokes and drinking (Tara faked her drinking to keep a sober eye on things), the night started to wrap up. Tara asked Ted, "Are you going to get your car?"

Ted turned to her and asked, "What's that supposed to mean?"

Tara responded, "What do you want it to mean?"

(continued)

He smiled and said, "I hope that means you're coming home with me."

Tara smiled back. "It sure does."

Ted went out to get his car from his parking space. Tara, who waited for him at the bar entrance, immediately picked up the phone and called Susan. She told her she was with Ted and for her not to hang up, but to remain quiet as she listened in on the phone. Tara then slipped the phone into her pocket and stepped inside Ted's waiting car. Ted and Tara talked for a few minutes and then Tara leaned over as if to kiss him. But instead of kissing him, she slipped the open phone under his ear, where he got an earful of Susan's screams. It took a moment for Ted to register what was happening. He stared at Tara and then it hit him. Tara smiled as she took off her hat and wig, and lost her British accent. "That's the last time you cheat on a friend of mine."

This time, Susan and Ted's breakup was final. Susan moved on and found happiness with a husband and children.

I decided to find out what being a PI was all about. I got in touch with Gary S. DeFinis, a licensed private investigator and the director of investigations at Philadelphia Surveillance Company in Philadelphia. We met at his usual wake-up call: six A.M. He had a hot coffee waiting for me in his dark van when he picked me up.

The first thing I noticed were the black curtains covering all of the van windows behind the driver's and passenger's seats. I was glad I had decided to change my outfit from a bright orange shirt to a black tee, especially when he explained that when people look into the van, they should only see darkness.

You have to avoid all possibilities of getting "burned" or "made," PI lingo for "caught." But Gary also admitted that "*all* PIs get made at least once.*"

First, Gary set his odometer to zero and filmed it with his video camera, so that the client could see what he was paying for mileage-wise, and also what time Gary left for work. The next step was to shoot the location of the stakeout, with the time visible. Gary said he doesn't need a still camera since he can always download stills from the video, and the video lays out a timeline and story of the entire day for the client.

I asked about payments and he said they vary, depending on whether people hire him directly or he's been commissioned by another PI agency. An average rate for his expertise is roughly $75 an hour, plus expenses such as research (database reports, motor vehicle records), phone and address information, tolls, parking meters, administrative or clerical fees, and so on.

Gary started professional PI work at the age of twenty, and is now in his late thirties. He specializes in stakeouts, something most PIs grow out of quickly, unable to deal with the tedium of having to sit and watch what can very often be nothing. But Gary likes it. He keeps things simple in his car: He has a set of binoculars, a video camera, a cell phone, and the knowledge of how to do his job proficiently. It's customary for a PI to call the local police to let them know he's there, so that if someone calls bitching about some dark van hanging outside of their home, the cops are likely to cover for him.

It was a hot day in Philly but Gary kept the engine running most of the time with the air conditioner on. He explained that PIs come up with all sorts of tricks to keep cool. Like taking an Igloo cooler with a lid and installing a battery-operated fan, then packing in some dry ice so that the fan will draw out the cool air. But, as Gary quickly pointed out, the condensation this creates on the car's windows isn't conducive to filming. Some PIs wear ice jackets. One PI even installed a battery-operated air conditioner, built right into the floor of his van. All things that are seemingly minor but become a top priority when you're on a stakeout in ninety-degree heat for a minimum of eight hours!

PIs will trace phone numbers or make "pretext" calls to determine if the subject is home. If the curtains are open, it's perfectly legal for PIs to look in from a public location (like the street or sidewalk). And it's all done discreetly and confidentially.

Many agencies' bread and butter stems from peeking into affairs of the heart. There are even women, hired by agencies, who will set up a "honey trap" and flirt with a suspected cheater to see if he'll take the bait. The undercover woman will casually bump into the allegedly adulterous man at a party or bar and start flirting away. Once the man starts to respond to the woman and indicates that he wants to have sex, he's left hanging. And the wife has documented proof of her husband's hand in the honey jar.

A PI's Case

A woman was in an auto accident and was suing the other driver. She claimed that the accident had greatly affected her lifestyle, that she used to be an avid runner before the accident. The insurance company stepped in and hired a PI: Gary.

Gary immediately found out that the woman was bullshitting—it was easy to follow her at six A.M. to the gym.

She'd step out of the gym an hour or two later, sweaty, and grab a cup of coffee before going home. When Gary would observe her house, he'd see her husband take off for work, their son for summer camp, and the dog playing in the backyard.

A few days of video footage later, Gary was again waiting for her usual routine: rise, go to the gym, and return home. However, this time, after she came home and her family had left, a truck pulled up and the woman approached the driver. They gave each other a peck on the cheek and then the man helped her into the truck. Something caught Gary's eye: The driver put his hand on her ass, to give her a boost. Gary decided this small action was worth a "tail."

Gary trailed them for eighty miles to a liquor store, where they bought what looked like a six-pack, and followed them for another twenty miles into the parking lot of a hotel. Gary went into the hotel and found a room with a good view. He set up his camera and filmed the two having sex in the car. And with a quick trace of the vehicle tag, Gary found out that the man was a teacher at the same school where the woman taught—they were both clearly making the most of the summer vacation. Gary smiled and shrugged, since this tryst was not what he'd been hired to find.

That weekend, Gary got a temporary membership at the woman's gym. He set himself up on an exercise machine, where he positioned his duffel bag, which contained a tiny video camera. Over the next two days, he captured her strenuous workout on tape: She would spend a solid thirty to sixty minutes running on the treadmill. Case closed.

(continued)

But when Gary reported his findings to the insurance company and was told the woman's lawyer was also her husband, Gary got the feeling this was going to get interesting.

There's a thing called "discovery," where lawyers have to share evidence. So the insurance company convinced the woman to come into their offices *without* her attorney. They had a roomful of lawyers, two TVs set up with videos ready to go: one of her at the gym, one of her cheating. They told her that they'd let her watch the videos alone so that she could decide what she wanted to do. Needless to say, she dropped the whole case against the insurance company.

The insurance company then kindly agreed to only reveal to her lawyer/husband that they had video of her inside the gym.

Gary explained to me that people usually don't use PIs for revenge purposes. But he gave one example of when someone tried.

One man called him to find an old college friend, someone he hadn't spoken to in a while and wanted to reconnect with. The client mentioned that this woman's mother lived in the area but he didn't want to contact her because she never liked him. "That was a red flag for me right there," said Gary. "It's always a red flag, no matter what, almost a hundred percent of the time, when a man is looking for a woman." Gary then explained his policy: If a man is looking for a woman, Gary will let the woman know and give her the opportunity to say if it's all right to be contacted or not.

So Gary located this woman and told her who was looking for her. Immediately, she started crying. She said she had had a relationship with this man in the past and he had promised he'd kill her the next time he found her. She begged Gary not to let him know where she was, saying she was married, pregnant, and happy. Gary gave his word. But he took the extra step to make sure this man would stay far away from her. He figured out where the now ex-client lived and worked, then contacted the local police departments, sending them a stalker alert. The police called the man in and told him he could never contact the woman again. The woman later sent Gary a thank-you card with an angel trinket attached, saying he was her guardian angel.

Roses Are (Sometimes) a Girl's Best Friend

PIs aren't the only way to nail your husband (I'm speaking of the other figurative "nail" in this instance). For example, there's a talk show called *War of the Roses* that's syndicated on various radio stations. It starts with a phone call from the studio, in which the host tells the  man who answers that he's just won a delivery for a dozen roses to the person of his choice. The man then tells the host who he wishes to send the roses to. Little does he know that his wife is listening in silently on the phone line. If

(continued)

he decides to send the flowers to someone other than his wife, the wife can jump in and ask, "Who the hell is Tiffany?" Chaos ensues.

So however you decide to get the facts, find 'em, get 'em straight, and then make the best decision possible for yourself. You're probably going through a roller coaster of emotions, so make sure you know how and when to get off the ride to stop and think. Don't let the ride take you into loops you won't be able to get out of. Instead, let's get to the spicy and exotic stuff in the pages ahead.

Chapter 3

COURTING ADULTERY

Life being what it is, one dreams of revenge.—Paul Gauguin

So you've confirmed that the bastard who wasted the last few years of your life has been cheating on you or is about to kick you to the curb. That all the times cleaning up after him, taking care of him when he was sick, dealing with his psycho and overbearing parents, listening to his problems at work or his frustration about not doing what he wants to do, have literally meant nothing. That everything you invested in him has just been flushed down the toilet, clogged the toilet, overflowed the toilet, and finally swirled down the toilet into the pipes of the hereafter.

You want your dignity back. You want to stop the pain. No, you want *him* to feel the pain, the same way you have. Actually, you want him to suffer more. You've found out the truth and you're ready to hand him his ass on a shiny, silver platter.

Revenge is an act of passion; vengeance of justice. Injuries are revenged; crimes are avenged.—Samuel Johnson

Now, hold up! Let's take a step back, take a deep breath, and think about what Plato might have done. Let's look at the lessons of history from all around the world. Some of these tales may affect your imagination, intentions, and decision-making. We'll see how people in other cultures have reacted and continue to react to infidelity and how they deal with cheaters. Hey, you may discover that you're in the right country at the right time—and the cheater will have justice served while you keep your hands sparkling clean.

When we look back at human history, we can find vengeance in every era. Steve Yoshimura, associate professor of

Communication Studies at the University of Montana, explains that "vengeance has a very long history throughout human evolution. . . . Mostly revenge is positive because it keeps people in line, it keeps society working the way it should. So long as people know that they can be punished in some way, for doing something poor, it'll keep them from acting badly in the future." He goes on to say, "If people were allowed to hurt other people without any potential consequences, quite frankly, I don't think that any of us would be here. If people in relationships were able to just have sex with whoever they wanted after they'd already committed to a relationship, long-term relationships would be a lot harder to maintain. Humans have incorporated into their societies the need for equity and justice and fairness, and it's because of those concepts that we've made it as far as we have."

Political Vengeance

Some politicians have had their share of revenge exacted on them. Arthur Brown, one of Utah's first senators, was gunned down by his pregnant mistress when he didn't deliver on his promise: to leave his wife and marry her. And Warren G. Harding, twenty-ninth President of the United States, suddenly passed away from ptomaine poisoning. Rumor has it that his wife poisoned him since she knew he liked to play in the various White House rooms with women other than her.

Throughout its relatively short history, the United States has had many laws on adultery. During colonial times, adulterous behavior triggered harsh penalties, such as flogging, exile, or even death. In 1913, Criminal Code 316 stated, "Whoever shall commit adultery shall be imprisoned not more than three years; and when the act is committed between a married woman and a man who is unmarried, both parties to such act shall be deemed guilty of adultery; and when such act is committed between a married man and a woman who is unmarried, the man shall be deemed guilty of adultery." Flogging a man in the public square for banging his babysitter doesn't happen today, of course, but infidelity is still used as grounds for divorce in various states.

While few people are charged with adultery in the courts these days, there are still laws in place that make it a crime. Public opinion is divided on this subject. According to one Time-CNN poll, 61 percent of Americans thought adultery shouldn't be a crime, while 35 percent thought it should. Some recent research indicates that in states such as Massachusetts and Michigan, adultery is a felony, while in most other states adultery is a misdemeanor, and punishments vary. But no matter where you live, adultery may affect the outcome of your divorce case.

Feeling Affectionate

In 2007, a husband in Illinois sued another man for stealing his wife's "affections"—and even got a judge to side with him, having the man pay $4,802 as punishment. How? He tapped into a state law that lets spouses seek damages for alienation of affection. Thing was, the woman at the center of this case said her husband was the one who wanted her to have sex with other men in order to add spice to their relationship. One of those men happened to be the accused—someone she started to have feelings for. Feelings she apparently had already lost for her husband a while back.

Even though Americans today have become much more tolerant about almost all areas of sexual behavior, cheating is still looked down upon. According to Pamela Druckerman's 2007 article in *The Financial Times*, "The Cheat Is On—A Look at Adultery Around the World," Americans have in fact become less forgiving about adultery. She reported that in 1973, 70 percent of Americans said affairs were "always wrong"; by 1980, that number had jumped to over 80 percent. A 2006 Gallup poll revealed that Americans were more accepting of polygamy or human cloning than they were of infidelity.

Girl on Girl

After Ellen DeGeneres allegedly dumped her girlfriend of four years, Alexandra Hedison, for actress Portia de Rossi, Hedison was supposedly planning a double whammy: take palimony action against DeGeneres and sue de Rossi for "alienation of affection"—a legal phrase that goes way back to the days when seducing a spouse was thought to be theft. Whatever happened with all that, one thing's for sure: Hedison would've had to prove that things were down and dirty between DeGeneres and de Rossi in one of the states that actually recognizes the law, like Hawaii and South Dakota. Hope neither was a favorite vacay spot for one of the De's!

So, let's travel back to the beginning of time. You know the man (Moses), you know the place (Mount Sinai), and you know the commandment: "Thou shalt not commit adultery." Jewish law held that both parties who committed the crime of adultery were to be put to death. Simple; effective. The Egyptians took a different route: The man was whipped a thousand times with rods and the woman's nose was sliced off. The Greeks plucked out the eyes of adulterers, and the Romans made sure adulterers were either banished—after cutting off their ears and noses—stitched up in sacks and thrown into the sea, or burned to ashes. The Saxons burned the adulteress, put a gibbet over her ashes, and then hung the adulterer over it. Decorative!

One of the first written laws on revenge was in the Code of Hammurabi: "An eye for an eye, a tooth for a tooth." Translation: Let the punishment fit the crime. Don't forget Mahatma Gandhi's response to that: "An eye for an eye makes the whole world blind."

In the Code of the Ur-nammu (circa 2200 B.C.), if a wife was accused of adultery by a man who was not her husband, she had to convince everyone she was innocent by doing things like leaping into a river. If she was guilty, she drowned; if she survived, her accuser had to cough up twenty shekels of silver to . . . her husband. The Euphrates River was booked for swimming lessons.

The Old Testament's Numbers 5:12-31 talked about a ritual to find out if a wife had been cheating. She and her husband would go to a priest and make an offering of barley meal over a tabernacle floor. Then he would take some holy water in a clay jar and put some dust from the tabernacle floor into the water. The woman would have to drink the water while he chanted. If she was guilty, things would happen, like her stomach blowing up and her thighs shrinking. If she was innocent, nothing would happen. Oh, and it didn't matter that it was thought that if she was pregnant at the time, she could lose the baby as a result of this curse. And when it came to the woman suspecting her hubby of cheating, magically, there was no test available. Can you say, "Bullshit"?

Painting the World Red

The Scarlett Letter, by Nathaniel Hawthorne (published in 1850), is one of the most famous American books about adultery. The heroine, Hester Prynne, is forced to wear the letter *A* on her bosom after she gives birth to a child produced by her illicit relationship. It's a tale that demonstrates the cruelty of Puritanical mores in colonial New England, but it also demonstrates how public humiliation was an effective deterrent.

The Leviticus 20:10 punishment for adultery spared neither party: "And the man that committeth adultery with another man's wife, the adulterer and the adulteress shall be put to death." You're both going down for that little party.

Sniffing Out Adultery

Adultery, the art of misbehaving genitally, has been frowned upon by human societies throughout history. The punishments typically meted out for this sexual malpractice range

(continued)

from the obvious and straight-to-the-point practice of chopping off the offending genitalia, to the seemingly more subtle act of mutilating or amputating an adulterer's nose. However, nasal dismemberment, which on first sight may not appear to be a punishment that fits the crime, is, historians and anthropologists record, a surprisingly common penalty for enjoying the pleasures of sex with someone other than your spouse.— Catherine Blackledge, *The Story of V: A Natural History of Female Sexuality*

In ancient Rome, Empress Messalina, wife of the Roman emperor Claudius, was quite the nymphomaniac. Her unsuspecting husband had no idea about the countless affairs she had. She ended up falling for Gaius Silius, a consul-designate who was also known as the hottest guy in all of Rome. She got him to conspire with her to kill her husband. She almost got away with it, but Claudius finally caught wind of what was going on and had her slain.

Greek mythology is full of passionate revenge. One example is detailed in Homer's *The Odyssey*, of Hephaestus, the smith and craftsman of the gods, who was married to Aphrodite, the goddess of love and beauty. Everyone told them they made a great couple. But they were both unfaithful to each other. Now, Aphrodite liked to get naked with Ares, the god of war, while Hephaestus was in his shop making the stuff smiths and craftsmen make. Only, Helios, little tattletale that he was, told Hephaestus about his wife boning the god of war. Uh-oh.

So, Hephaestus decided to catch them in the act. He told his wife he was taking off for a while . . . uh . . . on a business trip.

As soon as he left, sure enough, Aphrodite messengered Ares that she had time for a "quickie." Unbeknownst to them, Hephaestus had set up a net above their bed that fell down on them and trapped them while they were in the middle of lovemaking—think, a mosquito net that malfunctions. Then Hephaestus showed up with a handful of other gods to humiliate Ares and Aphrodite. They were finally released and both lovers went their separate ways.

But things didn't end there. Aphrodite didn't forget Helios's betrayal. Helios had been in love with a nymph—not nympho—named Clytie. So Aphrodite, being the kick-ass goddess of love and sex and passion, made him fall in love with the daughter of Orchamus, King of Persia. Her name was Leucothoe. Clytie became so jealous that she spread rumors that Leucothoe had been seduced by a mortal lover. The King of Persia didn't like the news. His idea of a son-in-law was a demigod or a guy who could at least shoot lightning bolts out of his eyes. He was mildly pissed and ended up burying his own daughter alive. Then Helios left Clytie, who died shortly thereafter. The Greek gods were like characters on *All My Children*.

> Every man wants a woman to appeal to his better side, his nobler instincts, and his higher nature—and another woman to help him forget them.—Helen Rowland, American journalist and humorist

As our species went global, so did all of our manic tendencies. Here's a glimpse into the international courts of passion.

Africa

In precolonial days of the Zande people, when a nonroyal wife was charged with adultery in court, she had to cough up something equivalent to a fine. But if she was royalty, then her lover was probably killed.

In Tanzania, the Turu natives got hitched and had something called "*mbuya,*" which means "romantic love." It basically said that married couples can cheat as long as they do so in secret, even if everyone kinda knows about it. The only time it mattered was if the husband walked in on the cheating wife and lover. Then, the woman's lover would have to hand over up to ten goats. And if incest was involved, it would cost the lover some serious cash.

Under the Kipsigis law in Kenya, a wife is a wife, even if she leaves her husband, ends up with another man, and has children with him. Those children belong to the husband, although he isn't their biological father.

In the Bangala tribe of the Upper Congo, if a married man and a married woman started hanging out together and refused to stop, the two husbands were obligated to switch wives. The innocent husband and wife of the adulterers had no say in the situation at all. Think *Wife Swap: Sub-Sahara*.

Uganda previously had a law that if a married woman had an affair, she was doing something that could be considered an offense and could find herself paying up or putting in time. But if the guy was getting his own nooky on the side, he'd never serve any jail time. Only in 2007 did the Constitutional Court finally get rid of the law because it treated men and women unequally. So now everyone can cheat and it's legal!

In Nigeria in 2002, one woman was convicted of adultery. Her sentence: to be buried up to her neck in sand and then stoned to death. But the court put things on hold so that she could finish nursing her thirteen-month-old daughter. Facing a huge international outcry, the court eventually relented, and her lawyers were able to get her sentence dropped because of a legal technicality. The woman went on to marry a local entertainer.

And one more example of Draconian judicial crap in Nigeria: In 2002, a man was convicted of adultery and sentenced to death by stoning. He confessed that he'd had sex with his neighbor's wife. The woman? She walked away free after swearing on the Qur'an that the only reason she ended up in bed with him was because she had been hypnotized.

Genital mutilation—or female circumcision—is one hell of a way to keep tabs on who's having premarital sex or fooling around on her husband, or simply to make sure she'll be completely deprived of any pleasure during sex (and therefore, less likely to cheat). It means that someone uses a knife to cut off or at least change things around a bit *down there*. They even go so far as to cut off the clitoris and labia, and literally sew up the vagina, which is to be loosened when the husband is ready for her. Some think that this practice, called infibulation, was initially used as a way to ward off evil spirits from entering a woman's body through her vagina.

All of this brutality, which can cause severe hemorrhaging, infection, and even death, has sparked campaigns to ban such rituals. If, in an earlier era, outsiders knew almost nothing about these practices, then today there's no excuse to have blinders on since more and more horrific details are available.

The Americas

In the year 2000, in Colombia, a tribal governor and his mistress were whipped with a knotted leather flog in front of the whole community. And, no, this was not a fetish—this was government-imposed punishment. Different members of the Paez tribe took turns lashing the couple. What did the governor have to say afterward? "That was the first time [I had an extramarital affair] and I won't do it again."

In many Native American tribes, a woman who cheated made things fairly ugly for herself. Her hair was cut (a huge disgrace), or her ears, lips, or nose were amputated. Sometimes, she'd get a beating to top it all off. In Mexico, the punishment was more straightforward: death by stoning.

During the rule of the Aztecs, one way adulterers would be punished was to have their heads crushed between stones. But they could get out of this mind-blowing experience if the "offended party" forgave them. And if the adulterer took things a little too far, by doing things like killing the adulteress's hubby, the guy would be burned at the stake and have a front-row seat at his lady's strangulation. Some big shots in the Aztec world, including the rulers, even had their own sons executed for adultery.

Asia

Supposedly, in Hong Kong, a wife has the right to kill her adulterous husband, as long as she does so with her bare hands. The husband's lover, on the other hand, can be killed any which way.

In 2000, Shanghai's courts amended a marriage law and made the punishment for adultery and bigamy harsher. This was due to the fact that crimes of passion were way up, accounting for half of the homicide cases in the city's main courts, according to the state prosecutor's office. Plus, there were suddenly all of these wealthy men taking on second wives and lovers because they had the money to do so—thing was, that money was coming out of public funds since the men were Communist Party cadres.

Mutual Revenge

In 2008, one couple in Cambodia took splitting their assets very literally when they divorced: The husband sawed their house in half after he decided he wanted a divorce when his wife didn't take care of him when he was sick. The husband managed to move his part of the house over to his parents', while his wife stayed put.

On the Nicobar Islands in the Indian Ocean, adultery got huge penalty points if it happened between members of different classes of people. But if the couple was of the same caste, the wife could be loaned out if the husband was given something in exchange, like a leaf of tobacco.

Have you ever heard of "sleep-dumping"? In 2006, an Indian Muslim man supposedly mumbled to his wife, "I divorce thee"—*three* times, in his sleep. The couple of eleven years was forced to separate. And the only way they could get back together was if the wife married another man, divorced him, and remarried her first husband. Sleep-talking can sometimes get you in serious trouble—or make things you wish for happen faster than you thought possible!

In 2006, Cambodian prime minister Hun Sen's ruling party decided to try to pass a law for anyone hitting the hay with someone other than his or her spouse. If caught, the offender could find him or herself in jail for six months to a year, and pay a fine.

Forget sleeping with higher-ups to get ahead in *your* career. Eleven women slept with Chinese official Pang Jiayu so that their husbands could score some big financial projects. But sooner or later, Jiayu and the husbands were accused of corruption; one of the husbands was sentenced to death because of the illicit scheme. The wives got together to bring to light Jiayu's own corruption in order to get him sacked, and they succeeded. Such sweet romance: mistresses uniting to save their husbands (after cheating on them)!

In the Burmese Empire, if a husband found a guy doing the down and dirty with his wife, he could, by law, kill him. But if the man managed to escape, even butt naked and only as far as the next room, the husband would be accused of murder if he killed him. Also, if the husband suspected a man of flirting with his wife, he could bring him to court and force him to pay half the fine that was normally paid for adultery at the time. In addition, if a man had sex with the wife of a respectable *somebody*, and then split, his *nobody* wife was stuck with handing over ten of her slaves to the *somebody*, or at least what those slaves were worth in money.

Speaking in Tongues

Indonesia has a huge Muslim population, which comes with some uptight customs. But when it comes to affairs, things seem to be pretty loose. According to Pamela Druckerman's book *Lust in Translation: Infidelity from Tokyo to Tennessee,* just check out the local lingo: A no-strings-attached affair is a *bobok bobok siang*, or just BBS, meaning an "afternoon nap," and a brief love affair is a *selingkuh*, or a "wonderful interval."

Australia and Oceania

> You know that the Tasmanians, who never committed adultery, are now extinct.—W. Somerset Maugham

A deceived husband in Papua, New Guinea, didn't have too many choices when it came to what he could do to his wife's lover. The law *forced* him to behead the bonehead who had bedded his wife. Oh, and the bonus? Just before getting "topped off," the condemned man had one last supper that was surely hard to swallow: He had to eat one of his lover's fingers.

When revenge was necessary, the Maoris had a group of people bust in on the cheaters, grab all the valuables, and sometimes even burn down the house. This pillaging of a passionate love affair went along with their saying "The woman for one, the house for the other." Now, if you were found flogging the dolphin around a high-ranking Maori's woman, you were simply eaten. *Bon appétit!*

The Cradle of Un-Civilization

Margaret Mead, one of the most famous anthropologists of the twentieth century, made her mark with the book *Coming of Age in Samoa* (1928). The book was a study of the Samoan adolescent girls' sexual habits and psychology. She also mentioned that Samoans weren't really down with monogamy and jealousy, and divorce was as easy as the husband or wife just "going home." Part of the success of the book was due to Mead's conclusion: "Romantic love as it occurs in our civilization, inextricably bound up with ideas of monogamy, exclusiveness, jealously and undeviating fidelity does not occur in Samoa."

However, many speculate that her study was more her opinion than anything else. Derek Freeman, an anthropology professor at the Australian National University, claimed Mead's book was flawed. He said Samoans actually *condemned* adultery, with punishments such as beatings, mutilation, or even death.

It was written in Lance Rancier's book *The Sex Chronicles* that Samoan men of the Southwest Pacific had a simple method of keeping their wives faithful: They branded them. Before leaving their wives to go hunting, the Samoans supposedly swashed yellow paint on the wives' forehead, armpits, and abdomen. Maybe making them look like Big Bird was supposed to deter them from sleeping around.

Europe

The Viking king of England, King Canute (995–1035), ordered a man convicted of adultery to be banished and the woman to lose both her nose and ears. Smell no affair, hear no affair?

He Could Never Get the Face Right

Sculptor and architect Gian Lorenzo Bernini had an affair with his assistant's wife. But when he found out she was also getting naked with his own brother, he had a servant slash her face.

Back in the day, in Cumae, Italy, a cheating woman was forced to strip naked in public and have the entire town hurl insults at her. After that, she was put on a donkey and escorted through the city buck naked. "Ass on ass" was meant to dishonor her completely.

In 1910 English law, a husband could divorce his wife for adultery alone, no problem. But if a woman tried it, she had to have an additional reason in order to obtain a divorce.

Henry VIII was famous for many things, but in particular for his six marriages. He married the pregnant Anne Boleyn in 1533—but she gave him a daughter, which wasn't a good move since he only wanted male heirs. She was executed for infidelity, as well as for other things like witch- 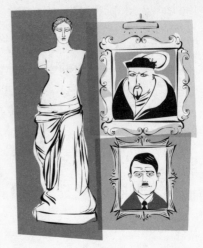 craft, and treason, in 1536. The five guys who "confessed" that they bedded her were also executed. In July 1540, Henry married Catherine Howard—she was executed for infidelity in March 1542.

According to Romanian legend, a woman's punishment for adultery was a little more than skin-deep. She'd be tied to a stake in a public square, skinned, and then left to die.

In France, the law accepts *"crime passionné"* (crime of passion) as a valid defense in a murder case. If a French husband catches his wife with a lover, completely loses it, and stabs them both to death with his ice pick that he just happened to have on him, he could claim *"crime passionné"* and possibly get away with it.

In 2007, Veronica Berlusconi, the wife of Italy's ex–prime minister Silvio Berlusconi and a former actress, forced her hubby of twenty-seven years to make a public apology for sexist comments that really pissed her off. In an open letter published in the leading newspaper, *La Republica*, she seethed about his behavior during a TV awards dinner. Mr. Berlusconi's crime? According to Veronica's letter, he told some women at the dinner: "If I wasn't already married, I would marry you right away" and "With you, I'd go anywhere." As the indignant Mrs. Berlusconi put it, "These are affirmations that I see as damaging to my dignity, affirmations that . . . cannot be reduced to jokes." His public response to his wife: "Forgive me, I beg you. And take this public show of my private pride giving in to your fury as an act of love. One of many. My days are incredible, you know . . . a life under constant pressure. But your dignity has nothing to do with it. I treasure it as a precious good in my heart, even when I make carefree jokes."

The Affairs of Court

The year 2008 was a good one for married Italian women. Italy's highest appeals court decided that in court, women are allowed to flat-out lie if they committed adultery in order to protect their honor. It's not clear if men could get out of the same sticky situation.

Adolf Hitler was rumored to have had an affair with his niece, Geli, who was in her early twenties. He was obsessed with her, and didn't want her to date other men. Even when he was busy with the likes of Eva Braun and other women, he'd keep close tabs on Geli. She tried to break free and date others. Then one day, she sat down to write a letter to a friend about her future plans, never indicating that she was trying to get out from under Hitler's thumb. But her letter broke off in midsentence.

She was found in her room with a bullet through her heart and the unfinished letter still on her desk. Her death was ruled a suicide, and one theory was that this was her way at getting back at her uncle for his mistreatment of her. But many people, then and now, have their doubts about who really pulled the trigger, and the odd break in the letter only reinforced those suspicions. Whatever his role, Hitler mourned Geli. He would lock himself up in a room for hours on every anniversary of her death, together with a life-size bust of her.

Adultery was a crime in West Germany until 1969. One of the reasons the government got rid of this law was that they were worried that the adultery charge was mainly used as a way to exact revenge.

Chivalry Is Dead

In France, [Benvenuto Cellini] had a long affair with Caterina, the model for his Nymph of Fontainebleau. He was fiercely jealous of her. He even wrote to a friend and fellow Florentine named Pagolo Micceri, asking him to keep an eye on her.

"You know that poor young girl Caterina," Cellini said. "I keep her principally for my art's sake, as I cannot do without a model. But being a man too, I have used her for my pleasures, and it is possible that she may bear me a child. Now, I do not want to maintain another man's bastards, nor will I sit down under such an insult. Were I to become aware of it, I believe that I would kill both her and him. So, dear brother, I entreat you to be my helper. Should you see anything, tell me at once, for I am sure to send her, her mother and her lover to their graves."

Micceri swore that he would be vigilant. But, of course, Cellini returned unexpectedly couple of days later to catch Micceri and Caterina *in flagrante*.

"No sooner had I reached that place than her mother, that French bawd, cried out: 'Pagolo! Caterina! Here is the master!' When I saw the pair, their clothes in disorder, not knowing what they were doing or saying, like people in a trance, it was not difficult to guess what they had been about. The sight drowned reason in rage. I drew my sword and resolved to kill them both."

Caterina fell to her knees and begged for mercy. Micceri made a dash for it. Cellini chased after him but could not catch him.

His anger cooled slightly and he thought it was best to boot Caterina and her mother out, rather than kill them. But they went to see a lawyer. He told them to accuse Cellini of having "used her in the Italian fashion"—that is, sodomized her. At the very least, the lawyer said, Cellini would shell out several hundred ducats to keep them quiet.

But Cellini would not pay up and the matter went to court. Caterina repeated her accusations there. Cellini denied it and told the judge: "If I have consorted with her after the Italian fashion, I have only done the same as you folk of other nations do."

The judge explained: "She means you have improperly abused her."

Cellini said that this, far from being the Italian fashion,

(continued)

must be the French fashion as Caterina plainly knew all about it and he did not. Then he asked Caterina to spell out exactly what he was supposed to have done with her. She did, in great detail. Cellini asked her to go through the whole thing several times. Then he told the judge: "I know that by the laws of his Most Christian Majesty such crimes are punished by burning at the stake. The woman confesses her guilt, while I admit nothing."

He also demanded that her mother, as go-between or rather, procurer, should be burnt as well.

Cellini threatened that if Caterina and her mother were not punished he would go to the King—who was Cellini's patron at the time—and complain.

"The little hussy and her mother fell to weeping, while I shouted at the judge: 'Fire, fire! To the stake with them!'" Cellini reported.

Case dismissed.

Cellini still needed Caterina as his model. He took his revenge by posing her naked and "keeping her for hours in one position, greatly to her discomfort. This gave her as much annoyance as it gave me pleasure, for she was beautifully made and brought me great credit as a model."—Nigel Cawthorne, *Sex Lives of the Great Artists*

The Middle East

Thousands of women are murdered every year in "honor killings." In such cases, a male takes revenge on a female family member who dishonors the family (that means, if she didn't marry the guy she was supposed to or agree to an arranged marriage, was raped while still single—without her virginity, she's worthless—cheated on her husband, or is trying to divorce him). The punishment? Death, in order to restore honor to the family. These horrific killings happen in Muslim communities in countries such as Germany, Brazil, and the United States. But, treated as a private Muslim family matter, they often go unrecorded and unpunished.

Bedtime Stories

A Thousand and One Nights is about one Persian king who not only had his wife killed when he discovered her infidelity, but decided all women were lying, cheating sluts. So how did he keep himself from becoming emotionally hooked and get to bang a hot chick whom he could trust was pure? He began a ritual in which he'd marry a virgin a night, killing them the morning after. But then one woman came along who threw him a curveball. She started to tell him a story that not only never seemed to end, but which the king couldn't get enough of. This also meant that he couldn't bear to kill her like the rest because he needed to hear what happened next in the story.

In the mountainous region of Waziristan, the punishments for adultery are as harsh as the weather. If you're a woman sharing bedsheets with the wrong guy, you're killed. If you're a man slapping the wrong skins, one of your feet is cut in half.

Flaunting Cultural Differences

The late Nick James, founder of getrevengeonyourex.com, revealed how he took advantage of what was acceptable in the Arab world while helping a friend get revenge. "I was in Dubai and a woman asked if I could help her get revenge on her boyfriend. Arabic culture is fundamentally different from that of the UK and the United States, and does have a lot of good points. However, women are treated as second-class citizens, and it is acceptable for Arab men to have multiple women and be physically abusive. Arabic culture is also about reputation being everything, and homosexuality is simply a no-go area. So the plan was hatched.

"This woman's ex-boyfriend was holding a business dinner in the Burg Al Arab hotel—the world's only seven-star hotel. So, during their meal, I dressed up as a very obvious gay man, minced up to the target, slapped him round the face, and threw his drink over him, calling him a bitch for cheating on me with 'Raymond,' and then I flounced out."

The Pashtuns of Afghanistan were all about exacting retribution *au naturel*. When a Pashtun dude was busted for cheating, he had no chance of saving his ass, literally. He'd have to sit in the scorching hot summer sun with hot pepper stalks shoved up his butt. Then he'd get some thorns pushed into his "noodle." Of course, the punishers didn't forget to kick him in the balls. Eventually, he died of starvation and exposure. When it came to the woman, she'd have to stand with her legs apart, tied to a stake. Placed strategically underneath her was a plant that would continue to grow straight up into her crotch until she died.

How to Make an Extra Buck as First Wife

In 2005, a case shook up the Saudi Arabian ruling family. One of King Fahd's ex-wives, Janan George Harb, sued him for "increased maintenance"—in order to continue to live in the manner to which she had become accustomed. She had lived in London for most of the past thirty years, after having been booted for not being able to "fit in" (she was born a Christian and felt as if she was in a prison when she married, and was forced to do things like have a few abortions a year), but supposedly remained close to the King. The King had promised he would always take care of her, but when he suffered a stroke, his relatives conveniently failed to keep his promise. The King's lawyers had already tried to hush her up in 2001, offering her money not to blab details about her relationship with the King—or the inner workings of the royal family in general. The King ended up passing away in 2006, but Harb got the right to take her claim for a £400-million share of his estate to the European Court of Human Rights. Then, she went on to draw up papers stating that as one of his two legitimate wives, she was entitled to a sixteenth of his £30-billion fortune.

In the early 1990s, Afghanistan's Deputy of Justice said that anyone caught committing adultery would be stoned to death.

Some Palestinian women have been forced to become suicide bombers as punishment for cheating on their husbands. One example: Reem al-Riyashi, a married mother of two, who got mixed up with a Hamas operative, who seduced her in order to recruit her. According to the British *Sunday Times*, it was al-Riyashi's own husband, a Hamas activist himself, who ended up driving her to the border crossing. Talk about supporting your wife till the bitter end.

Chapter 4

REVENGE AU NATUREL

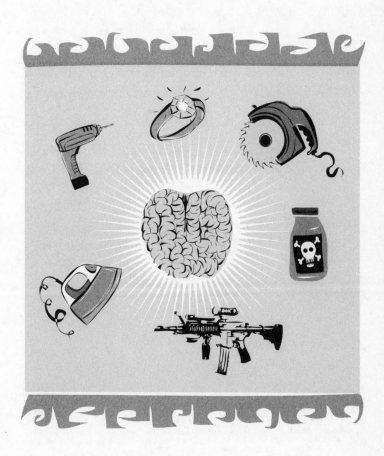

It [revenge] is sweeter far than flowing honey.—Homer,
The Iliad

So you want revenge, but you're feeling a little weird about it. Well, you shouldn't. Why? Because it's in your nature, that's why. There's even evidence suggesting that humans are genetically predisposed to revenge. Looking back at the previous chapter, this makes perfect sense. Why are there stories of revenge in every single country of the world and since the very beginning of time? The instinct is in all of us, no matter who we are, where we're from, and what time period we live in. So don't second-guess your feelings or feel bad about them—your vengeful desires are simply natural! It just depends on the type of personality you have to determine whether or not you pull the trigger.

The Number Shame

According to BAAM (the British Association of Anger Management) in 2006:

50 percent of adults and 87 percent of singles would take some revenge if ditched by a spouse.

20 percent of men would break the closest thing near them. [Stupid men.]

33 percent of women would overspend on their ex's credit card. [Smart women.]

50 percent of 16- to 24-year-olds admit they'd turn nasty if spurned. [Kids.]

One in four people would seek revenge on their partner if they were treated very badly.

Through brain-imaging analysis, science can supposedly show that people feel pretty satisfied after they punish others for being slighted; apparently, a biological sense of justice is rooted in our genes. The mere anticipation of schadenfreude (satisfaction or pleasure felt because of someone else's misfortune) prompts us to make sure the retribution is driven home.

However, there has been surprisingly little research done on revenge in sexual relationships. As Dr. Susan Boon, an associate professor in the University of Calgary psychology department, points out, "As for whether people do [exact revenge]: how they do, why they do, why they don't, what happens when they do, what happens when they don't, that we know virtually nothing about, based on my review of the literature." And it's only in recent years that scientists and psychologists have started to focus on the "dark side" of relationships—or "vicarious punishment," as some call revenge. Peter French writes in his book, *The Virtues of Vengeance*, that while most philosophers tend to view revenge as barbaric and taboo, many may not see the ethical values in vengeful catharsis. Basically, if revenge is shoved away as some horrible thing, we're ignoring one of the most persuasive ways to maintain moral authority in society. Think of it as a citizen patrol for moral and ethical crimes.

Gimme One Good Reason

A study conducted by psychologists at the University of Texas and published in the *Archives of Sexual Behavior* quizzed about three thousand men and women regarding

(continued)

sexual motivations. The result: Getting revenge was one of the 237 reasons people used to have sex. It wasn't a top reason, but it was still reason enough.

Stephen Yoshimura of the University of Montana says that he doesn't think revenge is studied much in academic circles because academics have this idea that "it's not a serious topic to study, and that it doesn't happen among mature, civilized adults. But the one thing that people who think that are forgetting is that revenge takes place among everyone. Anybody who doesn't think that it doesn't take place in academia, executive offices, or political parties is kidding themselves."

Where Does the Phrase "Revenge Is a Dish Best Served Cold" Come From?

Credit is often given to the eighteenth-century novel *Les Liaisons Dangereuses* (*Dangerous Liaisons*), written by Pierre Ambroise Francois Choderlos de Laclos. The French reads "*La vengeance est un plat qui se mange froid.*" Credit is also sometimes given to *Star Trek II: The Wrath of Khan*, in which it's used as an ancient "Klingon proverb." Apparently, a Romulon was tagging some Klingon general's wife.

From an experiment at the Institute for Empirical Research in Economics at the University of Zurich in Switzerland in 2004, scientists found that the region of the brain that displays pleasure, the dorsal striatum, jumped into motion when the

idea of revenge came into play. Some people had higher brain activity there than others, which gave the scientists an idea of who wanted to exact more revenge. "When people engage in punishment, the area of the brain that lights up is roughly similar to the area of the brain that lights up when people win on a slot machine or when they ingest drugs like cocaine," explains Yoshimura. "That's a very simple way of putting it, but it suggests that at the very instant that people punish other people, they experience to some degree a sense of glee and reward."

Another area of the brain, called the prefrontal cortex, does have some say as well, especially when there's some financial consideration, when people weigh their options of what is really worth doing. Kind of like a neural reality check or a little scale of justice.

Yoshimura explains that during one study, he asked people to reveal what emotions they had as they thought about their past acts of revenge. "The most common emotions that came up were related to sadness, anger, and remorse. Even though it's true that people experience some degree of satisfaction, it seems that over the long term, thinking about what they did makes them feel as bad as or worse than they did when they were first hurt by the other person."

It's a myth that the world is ruled by money. The world is ruled by that demon called revenge. From it comes all revolutions, slaughters, and wars. Family life and every erotic relationship is especially bloody, littered with corpses like a battlefield. A famous Eastern European writer had a wife, a lover, and a son, whom he not only hated but wanted to destroy. The son, purely out of spite, took his father's lover, even though he hated her. Then, for added revenge, he married her. Infuriated, the father, who knew his son loved his mother dearly, for revenge, divorced her, even though he adored her. Everyone was unhappy, but revenge was triumphant.—writer Janusz Glowacki

Does all this psychoanalysis mean you're crazy for wishing vengeance? "The best way to understand revenge is not as some disease, moral failing, or crime but as a deeply human and sometimes very functional behavior," said Dr. Michael McCullough, a psychologist at the University of Miami, in an interview for an article in *The New York Times* called "Payback Time: Why Revenge Tastes So Sweet." "Revenge can be a very good deterrent to bad behavior, and bring feelings of completeness and fulfillment."

Professor David M. Buss from the University of Texas in Austin puts it this way: "Revenge as one strategy . . . serves two related functions—one is deterrence (to prevent mate poacher from poaching again, or to prevent mate from cheating again); the other is a 'reputation' function, namely, 'I'm not the sort of person who can be cheated on with impunity.'" That's straight to the point.

> I've always known I was born to dominate your sex and avenge my own.—Glenn Close as Marquise Isabelle de Merteuil in *Dangerous Liaisons*

Many women admit to a sensation of euphoria when they're able to exact revenge on former lovers and husbands. They find themselves willing to lie, compromise a friendship, and even break the law. Are we all psychotic, hell-bent madwomen when backstabbed?

One Greek Tragedy

The Greek myth of *Medea* (the inspiration for a play by Euripides) is about one pissed-off wife. Her husband left her for another woman. So Medea had her and her father killed with poison. But that wasn't all. She took things to another level and killed her own children that she had had with her ex.

Raymond DiGiuseppe, professor and chair of the Department of Psychology at St. John's University in New York, suggests that women exact revenge on a man as a way "to teach him that if he cheats again, he's really going to pay a price."

> In revenge and in love, woman is more barbaric than man
> is.—Friedrich Nietzsche

Perhaps this outlook on women simply has something to do with "girls will be girls." According to studies, young girls certainly find ways to hurt others, but they don't bully them the way boys usually do. Rather, their methods have to do with *relational aggression* (a term used in a 1995 article by Nicki Crick and Jennifer Grotpeter), which is a more discreet form of aggression—and also a way to gain power. Think: passive aggression. The bottom line is that they can be the ultimate bitch, using manipulation, gossip, and social exclusion to get back at someone. It may not be in the form of physical pain like a knuckle sandwich, but it can scar much deeper and for much longer.

> Sweet is revenge—especially to women.—Lord Byron,
> "Don Juan"

This is not to condone plots that are intentionally ill-willed, manipulative, and destroy-every-last-tiny-bit-of-him-kinda-thing. And not all women work that way when it comes to scheming for revenge. If anything, Yoshimura explains, women actually tend to choose acts of revenge that are covert, while men are more open about them. "Women are typically concerned that the man not only be strong and powerful but also willing to commit to a long-term relationship if she's going to have children" with him. That also might explain why women are the ones more likely to take revenge by having sex with someone else, since for men, what might be innately most important is to have a sexually loyal female in order to avoid raising another man's child. Call it the brown-headed cowbird complex. Brown-headed cowbirds lay their eggs in other birds' nests so that they don't have to raise the damn things.

A woman always has her revenge ready.—Jean-Baptiste Molière

The Caller

"Jen" told me about her tale of delicious manipulation. Years ago, "Bill" and Jen decided to separate after eight years of marriage. The time was ripe in their case. The bullshit reason was that Bill had a job that took him to a different city every other week; the real reason was that they just weren't feeling it anymore. And the decision to call it quits was made even easier by the fact that they didn't have kids.

During the separation, Bill started to see a woman named "Karen" in this other city that he flew to for work. Jen knew about it. But when Bill suggested they try to get their marriage back on track, Jen agreed. Bill came back home to be with Jen, and they tried. They tried hard, but they were constantly being interrupted by phone calls from Karen. If Bill picked up, Karen would try to talk him into coming back to her; if Jen picked up, Karen would hang up without a word said. It was understandably infuriating for Jen, who wanted Bill all to herself.

She became even more frustrated when she and Bill came to the conclusion that it was over and that there was no sense lying about what wasn't there anymore. Bill packed up and flew back to Karen. Jen and Bill agreed that they shouldn't have any contact with each other—no phone calls, no e-mails, no nothing—for a solid two months, like "flushing the system." After all, they had been part of each other's lives for almost a decade and there was a comfort zone that was hard to get rid of. It wasn't as simple as ripping off a bandage.

But Jen wasn't finished with Karen.

One night, when Jen came home tipsy from a dinner party, she picked up the phone and dialed, adding *67 before the number to conceal her own number. She had no plan in mind, but there was no stopping this uncontrollable urge to be dastardly. Karen picked up the phone and Jen, quickly changing her voice into a much deeper tone than her normal perky and cheerful one, spoke up.

"Karen?"

Karen paused. "Jen? Are you all right?"

"Oh yes; just fine," Jen said sarcastically. "I just wanted to let you know how grateful I am that you took care of Bill when I wasn't there for him."

Silence.

Jen coughed and kept her put-on voice. "I hope he told you the news."

"What news?" Karen asked.

"You know, that I'm pregnant."

Gasp. "What?"

"Yes, I'm pregnant. I'm sure Bill told you, since he really hopes you're okay with it. We'll all have to work this out somehow."

Silence.

"Okay, I should let you go," Jen said. "Give Bill my love."

And Jen hung up, somewhat stunned at what she had just done. She got up and then sat right back down on the bed.

Suddenly, the phone rang. She quickly lay down on the bed, even pulling the covers up over her head. She picked up the phone, pretending she was sleepy.

"He . . . llo." *Yawn.*

"Jen?" It was Bill.

"Bill? What are you doing calling me? I thought we said—"

"Didn't you just call?"

"What? No. What are you talking about? We had a pact."

Bill hesitated. "I know, I know. It's just . . . well . . ."

Feigning concern, Jen said, "What's wrong? Are you okay?"

"Yes, I'm fine," Bill replied, puzzled. "Well, it's Karen."

"Oh."

"She said you called her."

"You're crazy. Why would I call? Wait. Is this some kind of excuse for you to call?"

"No! I mean, no, because we made that pact."

"So why are you calling me then?" Jen started to sound irritated.

"Karen said you called her and told her you're pregnant."

Silence.

"Jen?"

"Is this a joke? I mean, are you crazy? You really think I called and said something like that? I can't believe you would even think that after eight years of marriage. Wow, Bill. I don't even know what to say."

Bill was starting to feel stupid. "I'm sorry. It was probably a prank, some stupid idiot . . ."

"Yes, a stupid idiot. I'm really surprised you even bothered to call me about all this crap."

"I know, it was probably a prank."

"Or maybe Karen's making it up." Jen bit her lip, wondering if she had gone a bit too far with that last bit.

But Bill was clearly thinking about the same possibility. "Look, people are just strange. It could've been anyone. I'm sorry. You okay?"

"Just trying to sleep."

"All right, then. Jen, um . . . We'll talk . . . soon."

And they both hung up. Jen realized she had succeeded in planting the germ of distrust. She even called a mutual friend and casually mentioned that she had heard Bill and Karen got a crazy call from someone pretending to be her, saying she was pregnant. Her friend asked her, "Are you?"

Jen replied, "I don't want to answer that." Rumors spread like wildfire, and Karen nervously waited for nine months to pass before she could fully trust that Bill was telling her the truth that Jen wasn't pregnant—and Bill took a while before getting over wondering whether Karen had made it all up.

Women do most delight in revenge.—Sir Thomas Browne

The Other Sex

Men are not exactly innocent when it comes to baring the fangs of vengeance. They are more straightforward and overt about it. Even in the world's first novel, *The Odyssey,* by Homer, Menelaus, king of Sparta, launched the Trojan War when his hot wife, Helen, ran off with Paris, the prince of Troy. Paris was murdered, so Helen licked her wounds by marrying his brother, Deiphobus. But that didn't last long either: Menelaus still came after them and had Deiphobus off'd as well.

A brain study by University College London, published in

Nature, has shown that men may be more likely than women to want vengeance. When men and women were compared in these studies, women tended to have more sympathy for people who are going through painful experiences than men, therefore not feeling as great an urge for revenge as men might. And if it was someone they despised, men couldn't have cared less what happened to him or her, while women always felt at least a shred of sympathy. Men "expressed more desire for revenge and seemed to feel satisfaction when unfair people were given what they perceived as deserved physical punishment," said Dr. Tania Singer, the lead researcher. In general, men preferred physical revenge, and women social types of revenge.

> When a man steals your wife, there is no better revenge than to let him keep her.—Sacha Guitry, French film actor

But there's another reason why men curb the sympathy: Simply put, they don't have enough security. Why? Until recent times, a man could never be one hundred percent sure that his woman was pregnant with *his* child. Remember that brown-headed cowbird complex? That, of course, has changed with all the advances of DNA tests and so on, but who takes a test like that for no reason? And those things cost an arm and a leg. As David Buss states in his book *The Dangerous Passion*, there's an African phrase that captures this male fear: "Mama's baby, papa's maybe." Buss goes on to say, "Biology has granted women a confidence in genetic parenthood that no man can share with absolute certainty." This underlying, if not unconscious, notion gives women confidence, while it can stir up jealous emotions in men. And as Buss explains, "Jealousy is an adaptation. Jealousy is emotional wisdom, not consciously articulated, passed down to us over millions of years by our successful forebears." And this jealousy can easily be transformed into a desire for revenge. As Raymond DiGiuseppe states, men exact revenge in order to make sure a woman "knows not to leave. He has access to reproduction."

Keeping It All in the Family

"Jessica" was a college freshman at her hometown university, and one of the graduate-school science professors, "Jake," started to flirt with her. He was in his early thirties and seemed wise beyond his years; he introduced her to a sophisticated lifestyle, to restaurants and so on. But Jessica didn't realize just how much Jake liked her, and became increasingly annoyed when he kept begging to spend more time with her.

One weekend, he suggested they go away and she said no; she had a huge science project due. Jake told her not to worry, that he'd help. So she went away, and when they returned, sure enough, he did the assignment for her. But the irony was, her teachers failed her on that project—in the subject Jake taught! That was the last straw and Jessica ended things with him.

Shortly after, she got the school transfer she had applied for and left, fulfilling her dream of attending college away from home. But when she returned a few months later during a term break, she discovered that Jake had seduced her sister, wined and dined her so that she fell for him head over heels (she did not know about the flirtation that had gone on between Jake and Jessica), and then, at the pinnacle of their relationship, flat-out dumped her. Jessica's sister was devastated, and Jessica, in turn, felt even worse since she realized it was his twisted way at getting back at her.

Either way, revenge is something that both men and women desire or fantasize about, and it's been a natural human emotion—whether action is taken or not—since the beginning of time. Says Professor Kristina Coop Gordon, associate professor of clinical psychology at the University of Tennessee, "I think it's a fairly human impulse; not particularly a gender impulse." If you're pissed off, venting your rage and a bit of inflicted pain might just be the medicine that will help you move on.

Well, I can wear heels now.—Nicole Kidman on breaking up with her shorter ex-husband, Tom Cruise, on *The Late Show with David Letterman*

Who's Victimized?

When expressing all this anger and hurt, people often do things that are out of character. Some experts explain that this is a result of the trauma one goes through when he or she is betrayed. "We have assumptions that help us operate in the world. The world is generally safe, people are generally good, we generally have control over what happens to us. We have assumptions about our relationships, about the people we marry," says Gordon. "And a major betrayal, like an affair, disrupts those assumptions."

Gordon says people have similar reactions to those who go through traumas like rape or natural disasters. They are "hypervigilant, easily startled, extremely anxious. They have intrusive thoughts that they can't get out of their heads about the event." The ones who are traumatized do things like exact revenge in ways they would have never thought of before. Dr. Susan Boon says people in her studies gave the following reasons for exacting revenge: to restore justice; to give the other person a taste of his own medicine; to make the person hurt and suffer like they have; to restore self-esteem, public self-image, power, and so on. Boon also explains that none of her participants "suggested that they were taking revenge to benefit the relationship," adding, "We were surprised . . . we did have some of them talking about it as a good thing that had happened as a result of taking revenge, but nobody cited that as a motive."

> I'm trying to settle how I shall pay Hindley back. I don't care how long I wait, if I can only do it at last. I hope he will not die before I do!—Emily Brontë, *Wuthering Heights*

Going to the Extreme

Unfortunately, doing things out of character in the heat of the moment can potentially lead to devastating and irreversible consequences. "People are generally pretty poor at the calculus of revenge," states Steve Yoshimura. "And the problem is that the emotional hurt that people experience from initial acts of harm is sometimes so painful that they have a hard time thinking about what would be an equal response to that hurt. And when people are in that type of emotional state, sometimes it seems right to physically hurt the other person, and in some cases, to murder him. In retrospect, if we ask these people whether or not that was the right choice, I'm pretty sure that they would say no. It's just that at the moment, that felt like the only thing they could do to make the situation seem right or fair."

David Buss put it succinctly in *The Dangerous Passion*: "Jealousy, the dangerous passion spurred by infidelity or desertion, unleashes a fury against the partner or interloper unrivaled by any other emotion. Sometimes it results in dead bodies."

All About the Glove

O. J. Simpson's ex-wife, Nicole Brown, was found dead, with her throat slashed, along with her friend, Ronald Goldman. O. J. was charged with the crime, but was acquitted and then had the gall to write a book titled *If I Did It*.

Sometimes people threaten to kill someone, without actually physically doing so. The results are "trumped up charges of domestic violence," says Raymond DiGiuseppe, explaining that he realizes this may sound politically incorrect. However, if a woman calls the police to say she fears a man, she gets an order of protection and, according to DiGiuseppe, she pretty much has him "by the short hairs": "I [knew] a guy who had an order of protection and who used to meet his sister for dinner at a restaurant. So his wife was at the back of this restaurant and when he left, [she] started yelling and screaming and had people call the police. He actually served fourteen days in jail. But while he was locked up, he told his attorney there was a camera in this restaurant [that] shows he comes in with his sister, gets up and leaves, and never goes near the wife."

The Reality of Rejection

In 2007, a Spanish reality show that focused on mending broken relationships brought together a Russian woman, Svetlana, and her ex, Ricardo. He got down on his knee for all the viewers to see and proposed to her, begging her to marry him. She said no. A few days later, she was found stabbed to death. Turns out Ricardo, a butcher, had already been in prison for abusing her—and was found guilty of turning a knife on her.

DiGiuseppe also recounts the case of one woman who had her ex-husband, who was living with someone else, arrested approximately ten times over six months. Her complaints included that he killed the dog; however, the police discovered that the family dog had died of old age. Yet her accusations were ultimately successful because each time, he'd get in trouble. By the time he got witnesses to vouch for where he was the night the dog died, he had already been in jail. "It's a very effective procedure and I've never seen it fail because the courts are not going to take a risk," says DiGiuseppe.

Comin' Round the Corner

Phyllis Nelson of Iowa claimed that her husband of thirty-three years, with whom she was in the middle of a divorce, accidentally walked into the knife she was holding and—oops!—she killed him. She and her hubby were fighting about his cliché affair with his secretary.

Despite some actions that are completely out of character, the "victim" (if you want to grace that lying, cheating %*$&# with such a title) is sometimes able to recognize and move past your momentary madness, especially when he realizes why it occurred in the first place—because of him! Gordon recalls one woman, a petite kindergarten teacher who literally became violent with her husband immediately after she found out about his affair. She punched and hit him. She said she had never been like that before, nor has she been since.

Kicking Some Judo Butt!

"Diana" decided, against her boyfriend's wishes, to take judo lessons with him so that they could have more quality time together. He was against it since he claimed she was too fragile.

Diana was already in good shape coming into the class, and it soon became apparent that she had a knack for judo. Meanwhile, her boyfriend, "Jack," often found himself having trouble keeping up. As a result, he started to become increasingly distant from Diana, and they were actually spending more time apart after classes rather than spending more time together.

Soon enough, Diana found out that Jack was cheating on her. First through a friend who saw him with another girl at a bar, and again when Diana found a bra in his apartment. She confronted him and he admitted that he was seeing someone else, someone who understood the difference between girl stuff and guy stuff, who understood that he needed his

(continued)

own space for things like judo. He then had the audacity to suggest that Diana quit the class so that things wouldn't be awkward.

Instead of succumbing to the pain and tears of the breakup, Diana got angry. She decided to stay in the class and not let things bother her, like the new girl swinging by to pick up Jack.

The time came for an in-class tournament, and Diana asked her sensei if she could fight a male in order to reach the next belt level. The sensei knew what was going on, so he paired her with Jack. At 165 pounds, he outweighed her by forty pounds, but she managed to beat him—humiliating him in front of the class and his new girl, who came just in time to witness her guy getting whipped around the mat by his ex-girlfriend. And despite the fact that Jack was steaming, the sensei made him bow in respect to Diana after the match. Diana couldn't have asked for a better way to get back at him.

"My ex never returned to class, never took his belt test," said Diana. "I heard that his girlfriend had broken up with him, and I like to think it had something to do with that day when I took revenge on my cheating, sexist ex-boyfriend on the judo mat. It's also important for women to know they don't have to be 'she-males' to be strong—they can be feminine and sexy and still kick butt!"

What's It All About?

This is not to imply that all people who get dumped or cheated on seek vengeance—or even if they do, that they go to such lengths to get even. As a matter of fact, there are studies that show that "acts of revenge are not common dimensions to a relationship breakup and, overall, any report of them sensationalizes what happens when two people separate," says assistant professor of psychology David A. Sbarra of the University of Arizona. But that doesn't mean the thought hasn't crossed many people's minds. Gordon suggests that there are some positive aspects to exacting revenge, "in some ways, in getting your own back, feeling stronger, feeling that you're showing yourself that you're not powerless, that you're getting some sense of control . . . that you want to say what happened was wrong and should not have happened," adding, "I think that's a very healthy thing for people to do."

The Ring of Fire

A viral joke spun around cyberspace about a man who had to go to the hospital to have his wedding ring removed from his penis. The obvious question: How'd it get there? Turns out, his lover (who didn't realize she was a mistress) got pissed about finding the ring and used petroleum jelly to get it on his noodle while he slept.

What's worse? Your mistress putting your wedding band on your penis, explaining to your wife how the ring got on your tonker, or discovering that your penis fits through your wedding ring?

Yoshimura goes further into the importance of comprehending revenge, rather than just labeling it as some crazy behavior. "It's important to understand why people engage in [revenge] so we can help people in the future, or at least explain why we act in the ways that we do." Yoshimura likens this ability to understand to how researchers, for example, want to publish information on how explosive devices work. It's about understanding these potentially harmful actions so that they can be stopped in the future. "One of the benefits of research and public discussion about revenge," says Yoshimura when asked about the ethics of listing revenge stories and ideas—like in this book—"is that it gets people talking about it, and once we can understand why it happens, we can develop the cultural norms to decide to push people into positive directions rather than negative directions."

But let's be perfectly frank: Who doesn't want to live vicariously through what a number of "creative" people have done in order to get at someone? It's one wild ride that's hard not to watch.

> I suppose the crux of their relationship basically means to him that age doesn't matter, and to her that size doesn't matter.—Brittany Murphy on Ashton Kutcher being with Demi Moore, on *The Late Show with David Letterman* (Kutcher's ex-girlfriend also added: "Kidding!")

Vicarious Revenge

When "That Girl Emily" found out that her husband was cheating, she declared "14 Days of Wrath," saying, "I've decided that fourteen days is precisely the amount of time I'll still devote to that faithless and deceitful husband before I wash my hands of him completely." The fictional Emily paid for expensive billboards all over Manhattan. She handed out his wine collection to every homeless person she came into contact with. She put up flyers with a picture of her husband that said "Lost Dog." She pawned her engagement ring and spent the money on a private Pilates instructor. She laced homemade brownies with Ex-Lax and sent them to his office. She drove her SUV to Bryant Park and began throwing everything he owned—20-inch flat-screen TV, laptop clothes, golf clubs, etc.—out on the street for bystanders to grab. She spray-painted his BMW with "Hope she was worth it" and "StevenIsACheatingDog.com." And she even had the famous Katz's Deli in New York City create a sandwich in his honor: "The Cheatin' Steven"—a hard salami Reuben.

Of course, Emily and Steven were made-up characters, and there were actors who went out and pretended to be them. It was fun to watch a fabricated scorned woman with the energy, resources, and creativity to plot all of this (and let's not forget: The budget of a marketing and advertising team doesn't hurt either!).

> Billy Idol called; he wants his look back.—Jennifer Aniston on Brad Pitt, in *Vanity Fair*

Another way to live through others' revenge was by watching the ABC TV reality show *The Ex-Wives Club*, hosted by famous "exes" Shar Jackson (Kevin Federline), Angie Everhart (Sylvester Stallone, Ashley Hamilton), and Marla Maples (Donald Trump). Watching the guests on the show maneuver through the aftermath of their breakups gave people a whole new way to watch a broken heart mend. It included a revenge fantasy, such as throwing an ex's precious car out of an airplane. "I had a great time with the revenge segment of the show," says Jackson. "Even though it is nothing I would ever personally do, the satisfaction that a lot of the folks on the show got seemed to really help them heal—and I am not going to lie: Being in a plane and dropping an asshole's car in the middle of the desert was a BLAST!"

Creep

In 2007, Velvet Revolver front man Scott Weiland found out that his wife and the mother of his two children, Mary, had been burning up inside (and outside): She made a $10,000 bonfire of his clothes right in front of their California home. She blamed it on a medication mix-up for her bipolar disorder, but things had been shaky between these two for quite some time. She was released after posting a $50,000 bond. The incident took place only a few hours after the couple had been kicked out of a luxury hotel where they demolished two rooms during the course of an epic argument.

The reason we might identify with many revenge tactics is that most of us have felt very similar emotions when hurt. In his comprehensive studies, Yoshimura says he consistently found four major strategies for revenge.

The first is withdrawal, which involves avoiding the person or putting an end to communication completely. It may eat you up inside but at least that person should be hurting as much as you are right now.

The second is fashioning a new romantic relationship with another person—oftentimes, the other person is someone you (and, more important, your spouse) know, like his best friend or sibling. "It's not just hurting the person by saying, All right, this relationship is over because I'm starting this new relationship with this other person," explains Yoshimura. "It's saying that *plus* ending that one person's relationship with this other person. It's like a double whammy."

The third, but easily the most impulsive, retribution: property damage. Nothing says "I hate you" like urinating in the backseat of his Mercedes. Cars top the list of damaged items, but anything will work in this case, especially when it includes items that are nearest and dearest to his heart like wine, baseball cards, and movie collections.

And the fourth is reputation defamation. Aside from spreading rumors that so-and-so has an STD or is not well endowed, Yoshimura mentioned one case where a woman called the police on her ex, revealing to them his "chemistry lab"— or rather, his meth lab. He was subsequently arrested. In addition, taking things a step further, people can reveal that their ex has sexually or physically abused them. But if the charges prove to be phony, they can land *you* in the slammer, not him.

There are also less common strategies, such as kidnapping your ex's pet . . . The sky's the limit! (Actually, that's not true: A man was once so torn up over a divorce that he deliberately crashed a plane he was piloting into the house of his exmother-in-law.)

Yoshimura suggests that revenge can actually be looked at as a step toward forgiveness. "I do believe that revenge is a way of helping people believe that the playing field is level again. When they [do] feel that the playing field is level, they can eventually move on." But he goes on to say, "Once you start the cycle of revenge, there is a risk that it might never end. It could result in further acts of reciprocal retaliation that are even more hostile than the initial act, so it can be a dangerous game."

Dial-a-Dump

In Berlin, Germany, if you find out your man is playing with another woman's toys and you want to spring a surprise breakup on him, you can contact the "Separation Agency." For a mere $25, a representative will call your soon-to-be-ex and deliver the unfortunate news that you're breaking up with him. Of course, there are options: You can choose between the diplomatic "Let's just be friends" package and the drastic "Leave me alone" delivery. For an extra $15, the rep will make a house call to deliver the message in person (a Personal Termination Call, or PTC), unless the partner is known to have a violent history. Once there, in order to convince the partner that he's not on *Candid Camera*, the person making the PTC will reveal the contract to the partner so he grasps that this is the real deal. And if you're really spineless, for a total of $65, you can select the "deluxe" package, which includes the rep literally going

to your ex's house and picking up your belongings. However, be warned that the agency only accepts requests from people who have at least three "reasonable" reasons to break up, in order to avoid frivolous situations.

And in Japan, Breaking Up's Even Easier . . .

Can't say no? In Japan, several companies have gotten in the business of coming to the rescue of people who just can't pull the trigger. Called "wakaresaseya" (professional breaker-uppers), the agents are hired for the purpose of destroying relationships. They'll do what it takes to crush whatever semblance of love there once was (even occasionally using dicey legal tactics). For example, they'll set the client's partner up with someone else in a honey trap, film it, and the client can use it as solid evidence that he's cheating and she's done. But included is a lot of research, interviews of people close to the couple, and even tailing the person to figure out their lifestyle. The agents have even been known to steal documents and drug victims; they even put an unconscious lover on a train, and he woke up on the other side of the country. Boasting a 95 percent success rate, the company says some jobs can cost $150,000! You'd better be damn sure you want to say no before you call these guys!

To keep things less perilous, there are always the more mild tactics, such as the old-fashioned silent treatment. One University of Calgary study by Dr. Susan Boon followed a group of people, many of whom reported ignoring their partner or flirting with someone else (ideally someone close to the ex) as their way of "getting even." But why not up the stakes and have a bit more fun while you're at it? As long as you're within legal and moral boundaries, you're good to go.

So let's get caught up on some culinary dishes that have a different spice to them . . . and find out what tasty concoctions can be whipped up!

Chapter 5

A COOKBOOK FOR REVENGE

Revenge is sweet and not fattening.—Alfred Hitchcock

The Cold Dish of Revenge

Serves: Approximately 1 lying, cheating bastard
Ingredients:

> 2 shots of vodka (or other hard liquor of choice)
> 1 cup of proof that he's done something wrong
> 2 pounds of his most valuable belongings (the rest of his crap should have been tossed, burned, or given away to charity—call it "shucking his junk")
> 1 tablespoon of your spit (measure liberally)
> ½ gallon chocolate and peanut butter ribbon ice cream
> 1 hot thong he'll never see you in
> 1 bottle of Scorned Woman Hot Sauce by FireGirl (it's real stuff!)

1. Preheat your nerves to 450 degrees.
2. Marinate in your sorrows.
3. Shoot back 1 shot of vodka.
4. Pour the proof into a pot and bring to a boil, then reduce the heat and simmer.
5. Place his belongings in the oven and roast for hours.
6. Add the spit to the pot with the proof and stir until there are very few noticeable lumps.
7. Shoot back the second shot of vodka.
8. Eat spoonfuls of the ice cream, but don't overdo it.
9. Pour the rest of the ice cream into the pot, stir together, then remove from heat, add thong on top, and place pot in the freezer.
10. Once the mixture is frozen, serve it up to that lying, cheating bastard, garnished with plenty of hot sauce.

Often attributed to Shakespeare, the phrase "Hell hath no fury like a woman scorned" was actually coined by William Congreve in his *The Mourning Bride* (1697): "Heav'n has no Rage, like Love to Hatred turn'd, / Nor Hell a Fury, like a Woman scorn'd."

Preheating the Oven

So, what are some of the most delicious, sweet, and nasty ways to get back at a lying, cheating ex? What will be the most memorable or diary-worthy accomplishments? What will stick in your ex-slimeball's mind so that every time he sees wasp killer, your face comes back to haunt him?

The most admirable revenge I know is taken in Balzac's *Cousin Bette*. The target is Madame Marneffe, a ravishingly beautiful incarnation of evil who has ruined (taken to the cleaners) old Baron Hulot and is marrying old Crevel, a fabulously rich merchant, whose daughter Célestine is married to Victorin Hulot, a brilliant jurist who is Baron Hulot's only son. To complete the picture, Marneffe is secretly the mistress of the despicable Polish artist Wenceslas Steinbock, who is married to Baron Hulot's daughter!

This appalling situation comes to the attention of the police, the prefect of which is now the fabulous ex-

(continued)

convict Vautrin, and a scheme is hatched to right the wrongs.

A Brazilian magnate, Baron Henri Montès de Montejanos, also has been one of Marneffe's lovers and is furiously jealous of her. The plotters arrange for him to burst into the room in a house of assignations where Marneffe is in the arms of Steinbock. That is enough for Montès to determine her perdition: He has a servant infected with a deadly sexually transmitted disease that can be cured only in Brazil. He will have the servant sleep with a beautiful sixteen-year-old cocotte, thus giving her the disease. As soon as she is infected, Montès will in the same manner infect himself and sleep with Marneffe one more time—thus condemning her to an inevitable, rapid, and shameful death. Thereupon, once it is known that the scheme has worked, Montès, the young cocotte, and the servant all promptly leave for Brazil to pursue the cure. As for Marneffe, her hair and teeth fall out, she is covered with boils; when she scratches, she leaves her nails inside them. She dies in torment, followed by old Crevel, whom she in turn had infected.

The Hulot family has been revenged!—writer Louis Begley, on one of his favorite revenge stories

Here's a list of how some have tried to get their point across.

Juvenile Delinquency

If you're feeling more juvenile, or feel he'll appreciate your stooping to his level of immaturity, here are a few ideas that will take you back to your high-school days. While some of these ideas are actually quite clever, before you jump into anything, be careful that whatever you do, you won't have your friends pooling for bail money.

Some of these may sound obvious, but remember, there are many hurt people out there who simply feel as though their feelings for vengeance are best served with a quart of rocky road and multiple screenings of *Moulin Rouge*.

> A woman lost her husband to another lady. But the husband still had a thing for the ex-wife—so she set up a camera in her house. She invited him over, for old times' sake, and (after hitting Record) had a roll in the hay with him. The next day, she sent the tape to the new girlfriend as something for them to remember her by.—private investigator Vinny Parco, on one of his cases

"Katherine" recounted how she found out her husband was cheating on her after they'd had their third daughter. Their divorce proceedings had already begun but she was still hopeful that he'd beg for her forgiveness and want to get back together.

When he didn't, Katherine found a way to get even. She took photos of her family, including her ex and their newborn, and made photocopies of them. She then developed them into posters and wrote in big letters WAMMD—WIVES AGAINST MARRIED MEN DATING. To drive the point home a little more, she added the date of their wedding. She found people to put the posters in all the places she wanted them seen. The victim's friends managed to tear some down, but she was sure they put a dent in his reputation. As she said, "A good laugh can heal all sorts of hurts."

Just Desserts

Vinny Parco, PI, recounted a story about a pastry shop in a city neighborhood that was very successful. The couple who owned it divorced, and the wife got to keep the shop. Out of spite, the husband bought a store across the street from her, with twice the space. He opened the exact same business, a pastry shop, except it could hold several more tables, chairs, and desserts. When people came to the neighborhood, the first thing they'd see was his store.

Not interested in some of the guys asking you for your number at the bar? Give them your ex's phone number and a female version of his name or his sister's or mother's name (or better yet, give them his new girlfriend's number *and* name).

The Legend of the Dress

"Julie's" wedding day was approaching, and even though her parents' vicious divorce had made a huge impact on her life, she was still excited for her big day.

Her mother excitedly revealed the dress she would wear at her daughter's wedding. It was fabulously gorgeous and fit her perfectly.

A couple of days later, Julie was at her father's home, where his young new wife excitedly showed her the dress she was going to wear to Julie's wedding. It too was fabulously gorgeous and fit her perfectly. The only problem was that it was the same exact dress Julie's mother was going to wear.

So Julie explained the predicament and asked her father's

new wife to wear something different, but the new wife refused, saying she loved the way the dress looked on her and she wouldn't think about wearing anything else. Why should she have to change on account of someone else?

Julie was surprised when she confronted her mother with the news and her mother instantly conceded, saying she would be glad to change her dress. So Julie and her mother shopped for and found another fantastic dress for the wedding. Later, over lunch, Julie asked her mother if she was going to return the original dress. There didn't seem to be another occasion for it.

Julie's mother smiled and said, "But, dear, of course I have another occasion. I'm wearing it to the rehearsal dinner the night *before* the wedding!"

Your ex getting married? And he had the pit-sack to invite you, as if trying to mend things so that you can be friends? Here are some fantasy gifts (that'll never happen, but who says one can't dream?): Cancel the catering for the wedding the morning of, or cancel his honeymoon. Or loosen the stitches in the backside of his tuxedo pants so that they drop when he reaches the altar, miraculously just as he is about to say, "I do!"

Diamond in the Rough?

The French president, Nicolas Sarkozy, decided to screw with his ex-wife—by giving his then-fiancée, Carla Bruni, a diamond ring almost identical to the one he had gifted his

(continued)

ex-wife two years prior. He then went on to marry Bruni after only a few months of being divorced. However, Cécilia Sarkozy not only went on to be quoted in a few books portraying her ex in a very unflattering light, but she also married her New York lover as her own revenge. *Vive la vengeance!*

How about changing his license plates to CHTR4EVA and yours to RVNGER. Or there's the classic WAS HIS if you've got a car hotter than his new twenty-year-old playmate.

Got cash? Got a plane? Or better yet, a pilot's license? That's a lot to come by but some people are rich enough to rent a plane and do their own advertising. Like flying "[Insert name] has a small noodle!"

Down and Dirty Investments

When "Georgia" found out her boyfriend was cheating on her, she made sure that neither he nor his wallet was going to get off lightly. They had purchased a condo together as an investment. He wanted to move into it when they broke up several years later, and she said she wouldn't let him unless he bought her share. So she got a lawyer and made sure that he was paying the current market value—hundreds of thousands more than what they bought it for.

There may be moments when you're feeling weak after the breakup or scandal. Let's remember some of the good things about him. Remember how he was a giving person when it came to charities. You both served dinner in a soup kitchen on Thanksgiving once. You both delivered Meals on Wheels on a weekly basis. Imagine a film about an anonymous donation of your ex's priceless, autographed baseball collection to a school? Picture the kids playing with balls signed by Mickey Mantle and Roger Maris . . . (Wouldn't it be great if a local TV station came down to cover it?) Or does he hold season tickets somewhere? There are probably many underprivileged kids who would appreciate those. Or there can always be a mistake in the system and his name simply dropped from the next season's list of ticket holders.

Batting Dollars

When Yankees baseball player Alex Rodriguez (A-Rod) was rumored to be heating things up with Madonna, his wife took off to Paris for a "revenge weekend"—she allegedly racked up a $100,000 bill on his credit card. Talk about slugging away at A-Rod's wallet!

You've heard the complaints from other women. You may have even moaned about it yourself. You're a sports widow. He always has baseball on the TV or on the radio, or he's physically at the game. Did he drag you to games so that you'd understand—and possibly get caught up in—his obsession? Now, if you have good reason to suspect he's cheating, why not show him you did catch onto some things, like how to throw a curveball?

One person supposedly took full advantage of that enormous JumboTron at arenas and stadiums by putting up a photo of her ex and writing something along the lines of "John Smith, Tier 8, Row J, Seat 9, cheated on his wife with Amy, Seat 10."

A Sports Widow Gets Her Game

The late Nick James of getrevengeonyourex.com recalled a woman who was sick of being a golf widow. After spending years of dealing with her husband going to tournaments and overdoing it at the "nineteenth hole," she hacksawed all of her husband's golf clubs—but not all the way. She cut just below the hand grip so that when he'd next go out to take a swing, his clubs would snap and go further than the ball!

Is he taking a trip? If you can get to that packed suitcase, swap out all of his stuff for some nice, old, tired grandma wear. Depends diapers and dresses with daisies will be a nice surprise for him when he reaches his destination.

A Toothy Tale

One Minnesota woman allegedly pled guilty for biting off part of her boyfriend's tongue—and possibly even swallowing the evidence. He was trying to give her a makeup kiss after a fight; she obviously still hadn't forgiven him.

There are countless "improvements" you can make right in the home. Set as many alarm clocks as possible to ring at the same time all over the house.

On the toilet, position ketchup packets between the lid and the bowl. Make tiny holes in the packets first. Now when your ex sits, he'll get a red shoot-out all over the backs of his knees. Or spread Vaseline on toilet paper and then roll it back up.

Cinderella, 2006

In Romania, one guy got dumped by his fiancée four days before their wedding. He came back swinging, announcing that not only was he *not* canceling the wedding, but he would marry any girl who fit the dress and ring. It took only a few hours before he found a twenty-one-year-old who fit just right.

One woman claimed she replaced his business card. It looked exactly the same but with one number or letter wrong in his phone and e-mail.

Write About It!

Mary Jo Eustace found out that her husband of twelve years, actor Dean McDermott, was dumping her for Tori Spelling (who was also married at the time) after working with her on a Lifetime movie, *Mind Over Murder*. Eustace and McDermott

(continued)

had a seven-year-old son and a newly adopted daughter when all of this went down. Eustace decided the best therapy was to write a short story about it and get it published in a collection called *The Other Woman*.

Many people have made nice bonfires with everything that's left behind. Or dumped it all off at a thrift store. But some have even gone so far as to make it more fun and heated things up with some friends and booze. There have been different themed parties—from divorce parties, to simply "fuck him" parties. At events like these, place a photo of his face on a paper donkey and make sure everyone sticks it to him. Some people have even burned up all of "his" letters, laughing at his words before tossing them into the flames. Whether you're a guest or a host of one of these parties, it could be fun to film and photograph, then put it up online and make sure he's invited to the screening.

Burning Up Cold Hearts

During her split with Brad Pitt, Jennifer Aniston allegedly dumped all of his clothing at a secondhand shop in California once he left with Angelina for good. And according to several sources such as *Entertainment Wise*, she burned her Lawrence Steele wedding dress in a ceremony on the beach near her Malibu home, surrounded by friends, champagne, and laughter. Other items that went up in smoke: love letters from Brad, as well as his CDs and any other remnants of a glamorous Hollywood marriage that once was.

Of course you can follow what some may consider a "low blow" (although that could go for any of these revenge tactics for some people), and spread rumors about your ex. Dr. Susan Boon mentioned one story where a girl found out that her ex was running around telling everyone at their high school that she had inverted nipples. To some, that might be a fetish!

Moderate Maturity

Here are some instances where people have been a little more mischievous—and have potentially crossed a line. But when they erred on the side of caution, they usually just had a good laugh rather than be served a warrant.

Screwing with his clothes is a popular comeback. Like, cutting the inside seams of the bastard's pants. Slicing and/or loosening every other stitch, so that once he's out and snaps one of the seams, his ass is exposed! Or to get more to the point, some have just cut out the crotch area of each and every one of his pants. Or cut off one sleeve from every jacket he owns. And then throw out every right shoe he owns.

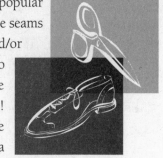

Patron Saint of Scorned Spouses

In 1992, Sir Peter Graham-Moon and his wife, Lady Graham-Moon, separated, but they continued to live under the same roof. When she found out he was having an affair with a woman who lived just down the road, she flipped. At three A.M., she tracked her hubby's car to the lover's home and poured five liters of high-gloss white paint all over his blue BMW. But she wasn't done. She then went back home and cut all thirty-two of his Savile Row suits, but not to shreds: She simply sliced a sleeve off each one's jacket. Then she gathered his most valuable wines from his collection and handed out all of the bottles to their neighbors.

Lady Graham-Moon became a celebrity—and the patron saint of scorned spouses to some—in England, and was supposedly even invited to appear on *The Oprah Winfrey Show*. What drove her to revenge? It was that her husband was having his affair right on her doorstep. She said, "I'm normally quite in control of my emotions. In fact, I am quite shocked by what I have done."

One man wanted to get back at his cheating wife and rubbed yeast cake in her underwear. He kept doing it for months and the woman's doctor couldn't figure out why medicine wouldn't relieve her of the pain.

Puppy Love

Nick James of getrevengeonyourex.com recounted the tale of the couple who got a puppy, and soon enough, the wife clearly preferred the puppy to the husband. Divorce proceedings went forward—instigated by the wife because the attention-deprived husband had dyed the dog's fur bright green and fluorescent pink!

Forgot to tell him some parting words? If your ex is into the dance scene and clubs, use an ultraviolet pen to write whatever you desire straight on his shirt and pants. Any black light will reveal your message!

Keep On Truckin'

"Trey" recounted how his wife started cheating on him with a truck driver. Trey was spending countless hours at his job, managing his bed-and-breakfast, and didn't find out what was brewing right under his nose. So once the affair came to

(continued)

light, he did things like pour vegetable oil into the gas tank just before the driver was taking Trey's wife for a rendezvous. She would call Trey half an hour later, in the middle of nowhere, having to explain herself.

Then, much later, when Trey had separated from her and she was openly sleeping with the driver across the street from the B and B, Trey, being a bit tipsy, took a stick and bashed out every single one of the lights on the man's truck. Although everyone "knew" who did it, no one could prove it—except for one person. Trey's friend who had just officially become a policeman was staying at his B and B for the weekend…with his mistress. He had peered out the window and was the only witness to Trey's revenge. But not only was he Trey's best friend, he was also in his own slightly delicate situation. He decided against performing his recently bestowed upon him duty as a cop and kept mum.

While Trey seemed a bit embarrassed as he revealed all this, he did beam and state with full confidence, "It felt *good*!"

One woman in New Jersey spray-painted the garage door of her ex's mistress with "New Jersey's Resident Whore: Home Wrecker Lives Here." If you were to be a copycat, beware that if word got around as to who did this, you may find yourself labeled the "Resident Crazy Bitch."

Another way cheaters have been flagged is going to their lawn and spelling out something "colorful" in weed killer!

Car-Kill

Raymond DiGiuseppe from St. John's University recalled the story of one man who, when he found out his wife was going to leave him, took his huge truck and ran over her Toyota, flattening it.

One woman Saran-wrapped his car so he had no way of getting into it without a lot of scissors, knives, and intense labor and time. Oh, and she had timing: She did it when he was on a date with someone at the movies.

Get Down, Dirty, and Sizzling Hot

One man recounted a story about his mother, "Irene." Irene was married at the age of seventeen to a wealthy man, whom she loved. She did everything for him, was his housewife, cooked, cleaned, but they almost never engaged in sex. She found it strange that he rarely wanted to have sex with her, but she still continued to love him, unconditionally and unsatisfied.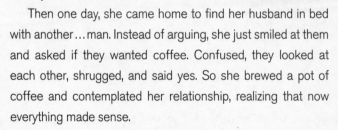

Then one day, she came home to find her husband in bed with another…man. Instead of arguing, she just smiled at them and asked if they wanted coffee. Confused, they looked at each other, shrugged, and said yes. So she brewed a pot of coffee and contemplated her relationship, realizing that now everything made sense.

(continued)

> She brought the boiling-hot coffee in two cups into the room, where the men were still hiding under the bedsheets. She confronted her husband, saying that she understood she was just a cover-up for his being gay. Before he could defend himself, she poured the coffee on both of them, then threw the cups against the wall. The men ended up with third-degree burns, in addition to some blistering on their man tools.

One urban legend tells the tale of the woman who knew her ex was leaving town, and dialed the "speaking clock" in New Zealand and left the phone off the hook. That's one expensive breakup.

Taking Revenge to New Heights

A Belgian mother of two literally fell for her lover, "Marcel." The two went skydiving, and she plummeted to her death at approximately 13,000 feet and 130 miles per hour. Her parachute had apparently been messed with by a fellow skydiver, who also happened to be dating Marcel, and probably thought three was a crowd.

Look up companies that deliver a product. Schedule a bunch of different deliveries, and make sure they all come on the same day and at the same time, when you know your ex will be home. It could be comical to watch him answering the door every few minutes for a new repairman—and dealing with complaints from neighbors that the repair trucks are tak-

ing over the street! Or simply post signs with his address: FREE
YARD SALE!

Burying the Past

In 1997 in Scotland, a sixty-one-year-old businessman
named Donald Pedler got pretty peeved, to put it mildly,
that his wife, Joyce, was dumping him to go back to her first
husband. So how did he get back at her? He watered her
rose garden . . . with poison. He wrote things on her bedroom walls, and ripped out pages from her Bible, on which
he carefully highlighted passages that mentioned the sin of
infidelity. But that wasn't the worst of it. He also took thousands of dollars' worth of her designer clothes and threw
them in the swimming pool (this included thirty-nine pairs
of Italian heels). And he found a nice hole in the ground in
which to bury her wedding dress.

Distribute flyers that say "I buy recycling goods! Beer cans,
newspapers, empty milk jugs, used plastic wrap, and anything else! Get paid for your trash!" Include his address and a
map of how to get there. Recycling is good for the environ-
ment.

Breaking the Mold

"Bruce" fell for "Katie" in college, and they spent all of their
time together, completely involved in each other's lives, for
eight months. Then Katie moved while Bruce stayed behind

(continued)

for a summer job. Off on her own, Katie started checking out her new city, boozing it up and smoking a bit too much. Even though Bruce admits he was no saint, he thought Katie was going too far. And he suddenly found that their relationship had entered the realm of "Let's just be friends while I figure out who I am." So when Bruce moved to her new city to be with her, he was kept at a distance. Their relationship wasn't lovey-dovey the way it used to be. After tense phone calls and meetings, he found out about "Gabe." Katie adored Gabe, and Bruce witnessed their relationship, filled with kisses and other things that reminded him of the way he and Katie used to be together. It was over between them. Bruce was left with nothing.

They did manage to be friends . . . for a while. He even celebrated her birthday with her. But the next day, she called to say she never wanted to see him again. A bit tricky since she lived next door. That's when things took a turn for the worse. She began spreading vicious rumors about Bruce, saying he was a liar, a thief, that he cheated on her all the time and was the worst boyfriend. When he went to pick up his vinyl collection, her housemates were rude to him because they had been told that he was stalking her. To top it all off, Katie wrote an anonymous letter to the co-op board, stating that Bruce had stolen the "slush fund," stolen marijuana, crashed her car, had sex with her sister, and so on. Thing is, the "slush fund" had disappeared while he was living *elsewhere*, he himself was the best guy to buy pot from, and he had never even driven her car. Plus, Katie didn't even have a sister. Still, she managed to get him evicted. So Bruce moved.

In this new city, he found a new gig. For $1,500, he became a dildo model. They took pictures of his penis and testicles, made a mold of it all, and even had a photo and a biography of him inside the package.

The company gave him a freebie of his replica. So he brought it home, wrote a note that said, "Go fuck yourself," and sent it off in the mail to Katie at her parents' address.

He hopes she opened it on Christmas day, in front of her mother, who envisioned her daughter to be an absolute angel. As Bruce put it, "Her mother's idealistic belief that her insatiable daughter was a virgin was dashed, and Katie, I'm sure, instantly recognized the seven-inch silicone shaft, thick as a Maglite, with a small freckle. In the end, I think I won."

Is he into his wines? Of course you'll easily find people who'll want to get their hands on every bottle. One woman made it more interesting. She supposedly took her husband's prized wine collection, carefully catalogued in their wine cellar, and let the bottles bathe in a bathtub. Not too long afterward, all the labels peeled off, and then she put the bottles—with no labels—back in the cellar.

Ash Theft

Martha LaFollete, of Ohio, was accused of stealing her ex-boyfriend's ashes from his grave. Supposedly, this was her idea of showing how mad she was that she hadn't been invited to

(continued)

his funeral, even though she had lived with him for five years before his death. If convicted, she could face a maximum of a year in prison and $2,500 fine.

Is he moving out? Did he send the movers over to pack up all his stuff so he wouldn't even have to confront you? One woman gave the movers his office address to make sure each and every item he owned was sent directly there.

The Dump

"Carrie" had been living with her boyfriend for a year and a half. She thought he was wonderful, only to find out later that he had been cheating on her with numerous people. She threw him out, which entailed packing up all of his things in a suitcase, driving uptown to his office, and dumping it there.

Then she received a letter for him in the mail from a former female coworker of his who was now living in Europe. Her sister encouraged her to open it and she did. It turned out the woman was pregnant and was writing to say she wished that the child was his (it wasn't; she was married to someone else).

So Carrie put the letter into an envelope and sent it to the woman's husband. She included a note stating that since his wife had no compunction about sending this shit to her house, he may as well know about it too. She felt that was the least she could do.

Zero Tolerance

Here's what some have done by taking things to a whole new level. Using these ideas as your own can get you in serious trouble, and you should not do them without thinking about them very carefully and obtaining legal advice.

Hammering It Home

Actor Teri Garr got back at her cheating boyfriend by smashing all of the windows in his house. How'd she discover the lying, cheating bastard's infidelity? His lover called to fess up, since she had found out he was sleeping with yet *a third* woman! When the cops arrived at the boyfriend's house, they thought Garr, whom they recognized, was the victim and made sure she was okay—indeed, she was probably feeling much better.

Sew in anti-shoplifting strips into the lining of his favorite jacket. He won't be able to walk out of a store till he's stopped and examined—countless times! Just make sure the jacket isn't from any of the stores he's going to.

Candid Camera!

One woman who couldn't get over her husband's leaving her and getting remarried would approach his house, smear dirt on her face, lie on the sidewalk near his home, and call the police on her cell phone. They'd arrive and she'd say he hit her, and all she wanted was to see the kids. Problem was, the husband had installed a camera in front of the house and caught it all on tape.

A lot of people have done this (but that doesn't make it right!): They've sent a favorite dessert to "him," delivered from "a secret admirer," and spiced it up with laxatives. That surely gave him a run for his . . . toilet!

> ## My Runny Valentine
>
> "Julie" had been with "Chris" for three years and then he went off to college while Julie, a year younger, was still in high school. When he returned for Christmas break, he admitted that he had slept with numerous other women on campus. They had a painful breakup but Julie finally came around. On Valentine's Day, she sent him a box of brownies, with a note that said, "No hard feelings." The next day, he called screaming and cussing because he ate those brownies—and they were laced with Ex-Lax. Julie finally got him out of her system completely—and he clearly got something out of his as well.

Some have sent anonymous cards informing the cheater that he was exposed to an STD, with an address on the envelope so it looked like it was from a doctor's office. One woman supposedly told his new girlfriend that he had an STD—and she ran right out of his arms! But if they had mutual friends, the revenger probably had to spend a few weeks of solitude herself.

Infected Relationships

One Manhattan woman, Stephanie Lerner, not only dumped her husband, Mark, for cheating on her, but sued him for $25 million for passing along STDs he picked up from his philandering with all different types of women, including prostitutes. She claimed he knew he was carrying the diseases and therefore should pay for affecting her health and work (she had to cancel a book tour). Sounds like he affected their relationship as well.

Another woman, Karly Rossiter, was awarded $1.5 million when she sued Alan Evans for giving her HPV (human papillomavirus). During their courtship, he told her he was free of any sexually transmitted disease; according to her, after he got her in the sack, he asked if she had ever been tested for HPV. That gave her reason enough to check, and she then found out that indeed, she was now a carrier too.

One guy took advantage of his ex's obsession with washing his hair every day: He simply masturbated into his ex's shampoo bottle. Ewwww! Another poured out all of his ex's shampoos and conditioners and refilled them with hair-removal products.

Time to Take a Moment for Some Mental Bliss

(Note: Countless acts of vandalism that can be exacted on his car are *illegal*—you can go to jail—so like most of the ideas and examples in this book, only keep these ideas as "mental bliss" thoughts that you can space out to any time of the day or night.)

Relax by throwing on those comfy, worn-through sweats and a long T-shirt. Kick back in the softest part of the couch, turn off your phone, and rest with an eye compress, cucumber scents flowing. Breathe through your mouth and clear your head. Then, take off the eye compress and try to focus on one point in front of you. Breathe again through your nose and imagine that point turning into the shape of a car. *His* car. Envision every detail of that car: the paint color, the aerodynamics, the interior design. Then imagine pouring bags of concrete into his car, adding buckets of water, and topping it off with birdseed. Or imagine filling up the gas tank with sand or giving it a new paint job—using his credit card of course—with cheerful colors like pink, purple, and neon orange! Or envision a knife slicing through those leather seats, a hammer crushing the stereo system, or your favorite colored nail polish painted on the detail of the car.

Now open your eyes, take a deep breath, and feel the release.

Plain Ol' Psychological Warfare

Messing with his stuff is one thing; messing with his mind is a different story!

> I told [Kris]—because that's the biggest thing in athletics; they cheat all the time—I told him, cheat on me all you want. If you get caught, I'm going to screw everybody on your entire team—coaches, trainers, players. I would do everybody on his whole team.—Anna Benson, wife of Major League pitcher Kris Benson, on *The Howard Stern Show*

If he's the type who needs to talk things out, or wants to stay friends since he has attachment issues (even though he clearly should have thought things out before he was double-dipping!), cut him off cold turkey. Ignore his messages and e-mails. If he leaves you messages that he's worried about you, that something may have happened to you and he just wants to make sure you're okay, wait a few days and then make sure to bump into someone he knows and look as happy as you can—and oops, yeah, you got his sweet, worried messages but you forgot to give him a ring since you've been way too busy!

The Politics of Marriage

In 2006, the Czech prime minister's wife, Pavla Topolanek, decided she was sick of hearing about her husband's affair with another member of his party; he even got the woman pregnant. So Pavla got a little political herself: She ran in the

(continued)

senate election against a candidate in her husband's party. Although she lost, she still managed to shed some light on her husband's screwed-up private life, and her husband publicly admitted that she'd gotten "sweet revenge."

Date other men, and be sure to spend some quality time with these new guys in a place where you know your ex's friends hang out. You can bet the house that they'll go right to your ex and tell him about seeing you out with some "dude." Not to mention that you'll have a chance to flaunt your new style—one that doesn't have you hanging on your ex's arm! Almost any man will steam with jealousy.

"Layla"

Italian-born model and TV host Lory Del Santo revealed how she got revenge on her womanizing ex, singer Eric Clapton. She simply had an affair with former Beatle George Harrison—whose wife, Pattie Boyd, left him for Clapton (some would say Clapton "stole" her from Harrison by doing things like writing songs for her, such as "Layla"). So really, both Del Santo and Harrison were serving it up to Clapton together. What scheme did they concoct? They spent three hot and steamy days in Harrison's suite, getting it on while he and Clapton were on tour together. Clapton didn't know what was happening right under his nose . . . but undoubtedly, he's had a chance to sniff things out since.

Stay in touch with his friends and family. Have coffee with them, go to the gym where you both used to go, hang out at the same art shows, and act as if you haven't got a care in the world. But, of course, when you get the call to go out to any of these places, play it like maybe it's not a good idea since you don't want to appear as if you're clinging onto your ex's life—usually, they'll talk you into going, saying that no one thinks that. Sure enough, they'll report back how sweet and happy you truly are . . . without him.

Playing with Egos

"Tish" was in college and had been seeing a guy. It was an intense affair that just as quickly fizzled. Suddenly, he stopped calling her.

She ran into him two months later, and a few weeks after that, he called her. She agreed to go out with him, in the hopes that something would develop this time. After some wine and dinner, she ended up back in bed with him and she was feeling sparks. But she decided not to appear so eager and she waited for him to call her after that. He never did. She was pissed and sick of shallow boys (never men) who didn't call back.

During the time they had spent together, she had come to know him a little bit and was able to figure out what was important to him. She knew that his goal was to become a filmmaker; he was a film student, and proudly showed off his short films. She even had to sit through a few of them as he broke down each scene in detail.

So one day, while Tish was hanging out with a girlfriend, the subject of crank calling came up, and Tish suggested

(continued)

they crank call her ex. Her friend called him, saying she worked for a production company that focused on seeking out and helping up-and-coming filmmakers. She went on to say that he had won top prize for one of his screenplays; that it had been submitted secretly by one of his professors. The prize? The chance to direct the script with a decent budget and access to any equipment he needed. She said that she didn't have all the information in front of her and he needed to call back and speak to a woman (whose name they made up) who would give him all the details.

The number they gave was to Tish's friend's place of work, and sure enough, he called first thing the next day. The friend was there to pick up the phone, and she acted as if she didn't know what he was talking about. He ended up calling several times, double-checking all the information he had. He even called a week later, just to make sure.

Tish never saw him again, and thinks he probably never found out who or what did that to him. But as she said, "I've never felt bad for the possible distress that I caused him, as I felt fully justified in passing onto him the large question mark of 'What happened?'" She says she felt so good about it that she even repeated the stunt with another guy who supposedly deserved it more than the first "victim." Her only regret: that the men never found out who did this to them or why. "But," as she goes on to say, "I guess the punishment does fit the crime after all."

Were there problems in the bedroom with the two of you? Did he complain that you weren't open to new positions and ideas? Before you call him out with knowing about his extracurricular life, give him one hell of a night of sex (if you can swallow it!), and become a complete wildcat: Break out all the handcuffs, laces, creams, and positions that make the *Kama Sutra* look like *Mother Goose*. This will not only give him a night he won't be able to forget, but will leave him wanting you again and again—and you'll already be long gone. (Although some men may argue that this would be the best breakup ever!)

Ladies' Lunch

Where does an ex–celebrity wife go when she's been given the boot? Well, she can hope to join the ranks of the L.A.D.I.E.S. ("Life After Divorce Is Eventually Sane") Club (aka the "Hollywood Dumpettes") in Los Angeles. Organized in 1985 and inspired by Marilyn Funt's book *Are You Anybody?: Conversations with Wives of Celebrities,* it was supposedly an AA group sans the alcohol addiction for ex-wives of celebrities. While bitching about how their famous husbands showed zero star quality when it came to their marriages, they also swapped divorce lawyer phone numbers, gave each other career advice, and networked over lunches and cocktails. Some may think this was an excuse for hanging out and gossiping, but the club did have other redeeming qualities: It acted as a philanthropic institution, giving to organizations such as women's charities and homeless centers. And as much as the members appreciated movies such as *The First Wives Club,* they apparently concluded that the best revenge was recovering.

If you want to take the high road, simply kill him with kindness. Be all smiles if you bump into him on the street, show concern for his well-being, even tell him you wish him all the best. In a nutshell, be as nice as possible to him—and even to his mistress. Show him what a class act you really are.

Now that you've found the right ingredients to mix together, *bon appétit*. But remember, always watch what you eat and don't overindulge!

Revenger Quiz

WHAT TYPE OF REVENGER ARE YOU?

Take this quiz to find out how far you would take passionate revenge. Are you merciless, indecisive, or just as whipped after the affair as you were before?

1. You've just found out your boyfriend has been cheating on you. You walk into his room and destroy . . .
   a) his mint condition Mickey Mantle rookie card.
   b) his computer monitor.
   c) his T-shirt.

2. Have you ever had revenge sex as a means of getting even with your cheating lover?
   a) Yes, and you liked it.
   b) You thought about it, flirted with the notion, but then decided you'd find another way to get back at him.
   c) No.

3. What would be the first word out of your mouth if you had to confront your husband about having an affair?

    a) "Bastard."

    b) "Bye."

    c) "Why?"

4. Your boyfriend of five years, whom you assumed you'd marry one day, suddenly dumps you via text message. You find out he's already started seeing someone else. You . . .

    a) take a page from That Girl Emily and put up billboards across from his office, home, and family's home that spell out what an asshole he is.

    b) concentrate on your own life and move on, although not without first making sure his new girlfriend gets a letter from you stating all of his "secrets," like that he had a hair transplant . . . on his chest!

    c) tell him you'll forget about it all and get back together with him if he wants.

5. If you had to choose one object to hit your cheating husband's scrotum with, which would you choose?

    a) A five iron.

    b) A boxing glove.

    c) A feather.

6. What's your first reaction after finding condoms in your husband's wallet?

    a) You get back on the pill and back on the prowl. Go get 'em, cougar!

    b) You ask your husband when he was planning on using them with you.

b) You throw them away in the hopes that he won't cheat on you if he doesn't have them.

7. What's your opinion of scorned women who have set their husbands' cars on fire?
    a) Get the marshmallows.
    b) He probably got what he deserved.
    c) Hope he had insurance.

8. What would be your first emotion if you found your husband in the shower with your best friend?
    a) Rage.
    b) Confusion.
    c) Sadness.

9. Would you break a law in order to get revenge on a cheating spouse?
    a) Yes.
    b) You'd push things to the limit but (hopefully) not do anything that was illegal.
    c) Never.

10. Your ex-husband had the nerve to invite you to his wedding. You . . .
    a) accept the invite but then pull all the strings you have to make sure the honeymoon gets cancelled.
    b) accept the invite and plan to go with the hottest guy you know.
    c) accept the invite and even buy them a nice gift.

Now, go and add up your answers. A=2 points, B=1 point, and C=0 points. After you've done the math, check below to find out what kind of Revenger you are.

14–20 points: Vicious Vixen. You're one hard-core, calculating, vindictive broad! You know how to get him back where it hurts—and how to make sure the sting doesn't go away. Not only will he never mess with you again, no one else will either! You're either doing nine to twelve months in jail at the moment or eyeing a tan pool boy in Aruba while vacationing on the money you liquidated from his Fabergé egg collection.

7–13 points: Mild Mamba. You've got it in you, but you're not bringing it all out. You have enough perspective to look at both sides of the story, so you're not sure if you're ready to just let him have it. Don't get derailed by thinking of all the good times you two had—or, for that matter, all the nasty crap he did, too! You just know that he'll pay for it somehow, with or without your help.

0–6 points: Pussy Cat. Some may think you're either a doormat or a follower of Lao Tzu. He might as well have a threesome right in your bedroom while you watch, break up with you while he climaxes, and then step on you on the way out. But even though these people are the ones who think you should embrace your inner Revenger, there are plenty who would say you're actually the strong one here—you know karma is going to kick him in the ass one day soon and you'll have blissfully walked away and already begun a great life without him.

Chapter 6
TRIED-AND-TRUE TALES

There are those revenge techniques that have added sizzle to dinner conversations for years. And for good reason. While some seem unlikely to have happened, others are popular lore that never seem to lose fascination—or inspiration.

The Penis Sagas

Nothing drives the point home harder than to focus in on a man's penis.

In 1993, Lorena Bobbitt famously cut off her husband's penis with a twelve-inch kitchen knife. She then drove off and threw the severed member out of her car window. The police managed to find it and the penis was surgically reattached in a lengthy surgery. Lorena, who claimed she was abused by her husband, served only forty-five days in a mental hospital. Apparently, she suffered from post-traumatic stress disorder, which created temporary insanity, and, therefore, she couldn't be held accountable for her actions. Lorena Bobbitt gained household name recognition (and some women even hold her up as a "feminist hero"). John went on to become a porn star, but not without trying to reconcile with Lorena, who refused. In 1999, John stated that he still believed Lorena was the woman for him.

No Matter How You Slice It

The band Tribe 8 wrote a song called "Castration Song #22" in reference to Lorena Bobbitt. Lyrics included "Lorena don't take no shit." Ballast, a punk band, took it one step further with "Lorena Bobbitt": "In the bedroom, the quiet bedroom, John Bobbitt sleeps tonight. / In the kitchen, the mighty kitchen, Lorena sharpens her knife."

In two unrelated incidents in 2007, women set their partners' penises on fire.

After a night of drinking and arguing, one Canadian woman waited till her man was asleep, dumped fuel on him, and then lit his penis on fire. She was sentenced to four years in prison, while her boyfriend suffered quite a bit of trauma—and probably had a hard time sleeping with anyone else again.

Meanwhile, on the other side of the globe, a Russian woman set her ex-husband's penis on fire while he was drinking and watching TV naked. Granted, things were a little tense between them: The couple had divorced three years before but had to continue sharing their tiny apartment due to Russian property costs being high.

One Indonesian woman living in Malaysia pled guilty to chopping off her husband's penis after he basically said she sucked in bed (as in: she wasn't skilled). Having been married to the man for seventeen years and given him two children, she got mad when he said she was lousy compared to his second wife! (Muslim men in Malaysia supposedly may have up to four wives.) Happily for him, the penis was reattached.

One woman didn't end up happy-go-lucky after she cut off her husband's penis. During a fight, the woman used a butter knife to cut off the penis. But her husband managed to use the same knife to stab her. Tragically, she died on the way to the hospital.

In 1936, Sada Abe strangled her lover, cut off his penis, placed it in a magazine, and carried it around. She also found the time to carve her name into his arm with a knife. She said she did it because it was her way of showing she loved him and her way of controlling him. She spent six years in jail; the penis was last seen at a pathology museum.

One Chinese woman suspected her husband of cheating and wanted to be sure he'd stop, so she cut off his penis. The man begged to get the penis back but his wife wouldn't relinquish it. He then drove himself to the hospital. When the medical staff went out to look for the missing member, they discovered that a neighbor's dog had already made it its dinner.

In Thailand, penis attacks are big. Between 1973 and 1980, one hundred Thai women decided to get revenge on their cheating husbands: They chopped off their husbands' penises while the men slept and threw the suckers right out the window. The phrase "I'll feed you to the ducks" is appreciated there. At least these men were in the right place: Thailand is a great place for penis-reattachment surgery.

Get the plunger. Kim Tran was so worried her boyfriend of one year was going to dump her, she took matters—and his penis—into her own hands. Not only did she cut it off, she flushed it down the toilet. Somehow, utility workers found the organ and it was successfully reattached. Tran was charged with a few things, including tampering with evidence, and jailed. The boyfriend happened to be Tran's aunt's husband.

Women aren't the only ones who know what they're doing with blades. One pissed-off husband cut the penis off his estranged wife's lover before stabbing the man to death when he discovered the two in bed. No, he didn't throw the penis out the window or down the toilet; rather, he threw it into his wife's underwear drawer. That's punctuation.

Urban Legends and Myths

As mentioned earlier, "That Girl Emily" became an urban legend. But there isn't always an advertising firm behind such acts of "public" revenge. Is it like a game of "telephone"? Or just rumors? Actually, who cares? True or not, they're revenge-book worthy.

A FISHY TALE

A scorned woman left her cheating husband the house they had shared and moved out. But she didn't take everything. When the husband let his new lover spend the night at his empty place, an impossible-to-locate stench drove his lover out. Turns out the wife had secretly packed shrimp into the hollow posts of the bed. But it didn't end there. Since the husband couldn't find out where the smell

was coming from, he packed up everything and moved to another home. And he took the bed with him.

MORE FISH

A jilted woman decided to take revenge on her fiancé's new car. She removed the passenger seat and cut the lining along the edge. There, she placed a fresh fish, and then she carefully restitched the seam. After a few days, the fish started to rot. The cheating fiancé vacuumed, deodorized, pulled out the seats, washed everything . . . but he couldn't find the fish. Not only had he lost his fiancée, but he lost his lover since no one would get into that car. In the end, he sold the car for half its value due to the stench.

Another woman was moving out of the apartment she shared with her then-lover. But she made sure to leave some fish behind—packed inside the walls through the light sockets.

Staying on point with rancid smells, there's always the "Milky Sock," as Jim Marsh of Deep Focus has described, if you don't want to get your hands dirty with fish. "You take an ordinary sock and soak it in milk. Then you hide it somewhere in your victim's house—preferably near a radiator or a heating duct. Once the milk goes bad, the victim will be left with a completely rank odor and no evidence of foul play except an ordinary sock." Let's hope he ends up wearing the sock, too!

MAKING SURE REVENGE STICKS

Ah, superglue . . . kind of like a Sears deluxe toolbox in one little bottle.

People have made things "permanent" by taking advantage of superglue to exact revenge. From supergluing an ex's windshield wipers to his windshield or the windows of his home and all the doors shut—plus putting glue in the keyholes! Or supergluing the toilet so that he was stuck—although the gluer may have ended up stuck in the can (as in prison)! Even the toilet handle has been done. People have also superglued the coffeepot handle, his favorite mug, and the fridge handlebar! And after turning the thermostat as high as possible, there have been stories about people gluing it that way so there was no cooling down—not even in the relationship. It seems like the only thing holding people back with a large tube of superglue is their imagination.

Did he betray you via the Internet? Were his fingers playing more with his keyboard than they were with you? Well, some people have figured out how to make his betrayal stick—by gluing his keyboard so that he couldn't turn away from the screen or gluing the ball inside of his mouse and even the mouse to the mouse pad. There are countless places people have laid it on sticky thick.

When one woman was sure her husband was cheating on her, she concocted a scheme that would guarantee his sticking around. One night, while they were still sleeping together, she waited till he was in a deep sleep. She then gently applied superglue to his penis and his leg, and held them together to make sure they would bind. The husband woke up to a sticky situation, and nothing could break that bond. It finally took a physician to make the separation, a metaphor for the couple since they did end up going their separate ways.

In 2000, Gail O'Toole of Mur-
rysville, Pennsylvania, treated
ex-boyfriend Kenneth Slaby of
Pittsburgh to a recipe of spite.
Although he already had been
dating someone else for months, he
came over to her place and spent the night. While he was
asleep, O'Toole superglued his penis to his stomach, his testi-
cles to his leg, and his buttocks together.

There was also the case of a sixteen-year-old girl who got
back at her twenty-one-year-old cheating boyfriend by first
getting him "excited," then supergluing his erect penis to his
abdomen.

Theatrical Revenge

Jim, a theater director and writer, started the "Revenge
Street Theater." With a team of actors and makeup artists,
they were ready to perform whatever was needed for
vengeance to be done, on whomever deserved it.

For example, when a bartender refused to cash Jim's
check at a bar where he was a regular (the bartender told
him, "If you want to cash it, go to a bank; I've never seen
your face before"), he sent a friend/actor to the bar to ask
to get his check cashed. The bartender repeated, "If you
want to cash it, go to a bank; I've never seen your face before." The actor protested, saying he was a regular. Then,
on cue, seventy-five of Jim's friends rose in unison and
chanted, "What! Won't cash a check for a regular cus-

tomer? Well! Well! Well!" And they all busted out of the joint, without paying for the drinks and food they had just ordered.

In another scenario, a woman whose fiancé was living out of the country was out with Jim and friends. She was known to be very cocky and a drama queen. Her fiancé secretly came back to town, got himself decked out in a disguise as a waiter, and literally turned into the waiter from hell. He spilled drinks on her, dumped the salt and pepper—annoyed her to the point where she was going crazy dealing with him. Finally, he said something sweet to her; she looked in his eyes and simply couldn't believe that it was her fiancé. She ended up locking herself in the bathroom and crying hysterically, unable to digest what had just happened. Even though they did marry, divorce was the result.

One suggestion Jim offers to get back at a lying, cheating, bastard: Have a friend who's trying to make it in the acting world? Send her out for her first gig. Get a *very* young girlfriend to put on a prosthetic stomach so that she looks pregnant. Have her go over to his office—ideally, time it so that he's in the middle of a board meeting—and have her walk in crying hysterically that she needs more money from him for their baby. That's sure to add a little something to his reputation!

Chapter 7

E-VENGE

Infidelity is an age-old sin. Piltdown man cheated on Piltdown woman. The Egyptians had orgies when the wives were sleeping. Even French Revolutionaries got frisky, fooling around with mesdemoiselles and mesdames, of course. Many centuries later, with huge advances in technology, cheating seems to be even easier. Next time you surf the personals on Craigslist or check profiles on MySpace or Facebook, there's a good chance you'll click on a cheater, or maybe you'll be the cheater. In the same way the Internet provides for one-click shopping and bill-paying, infidelity is also only a keystroke away.

Gone are the days when cheaters had to work the bars for extracurricular relationships. With text messaging, cell phones, chat rooms, and online dating sites, infidelity's a lot more trouble-free and strings-free. While the wife is watching reruns of *Sex and the City* on her iPod, the husband can be setting up a rendezvous with his mistress in the adjacent room on his laptop. Super convenient!

Technology has also become the kiss of death for illicit romances and impending breakups. While it may be effortless to hide affairs at first, the Digital Age also makes it easier to sniff out affairs as soon as there is a whiff of suspicion. Our lives are now recorded on our computer hard drives, office servers, and digital phone memories, so messages sent can easily be found or retrieved.

Down and Dirty Celebs

Soccer superstar David Beckham's former nanny claims she saw him texting dirty messages to supermodel Esther Canadas.

Many law firms say that a large—and growing—number of divorce cases enter into the legal proceedings evidence like e-mail, text messages, or cell-phone bills. While it's usually been his word against hers, it can be much harder to dispute an affair when e-mails and text messages that say things like "C U @ 8—BRNG KY" prove that he's straying.

Of course, there's discussion about what really constitutes an affair when it comes to the Internet. Does meeting someone online who's halfway around the world mean he's cheating? Does it bother you that he's spending hours in chat rooms or interacting with strangers on message boards? Or is it that you'd rather have him physically home with you—even if it means he's in the next room, possibly doing some one-handed gymnastics—than out in some dive bar, making out with the bartender in 3-D, tangible form. When do you think his online activity is getting too personal? Some statistics say that 30 percent of cyber affairs end in human contact—between the sheets. "Without splitting hairs," wrote the late Nick James, founder of getrevengeonyourex.com, "a virtual affair and a real affair amount to the same thing—you are being unfaithful to your partner."

In the February 2007 MSNBC.com and iVillage survey on love, sex, and fidelity, one of the questions asked of participants was if technology had played a role in their affair. One in five men and women said yes, that they cheated by using e-mail or text messages to set up times and places to meet. Some even met their future screws online in chat rooms: 8 percent of men found their mistress that way, compared

to 3 percent of women. But both men and women agreed that sending a sexually flirtatious e-mail to a coworker was basically cheating, and considered online sex chats or Webcams with someone other than your partner a definite no-no.

But all this technology does seem to have an upside. The same venue that has made it easier for men to stray might well be the best place for making men pay. The suspicious wives and girlfriends of the world are now retaliating by sending mass e-mails; revealing intimate details about their cheating lovers, whether they're true or not (the latter, of course, constitutes libel and can put you in legal jeopardy); creating personal Web sites that detail the end of the affair; or posting their ex's details on a gay singles' site or simply spamming their e-mail addresses. People are taking full advantage of the technology: text messaging, e-mailing, buying camera phones, and purchasing gadgets that you used to only read about in novels or see in James Bond movies. Technology has evolved to the point where you can walk into a spy shop and buy state-of-the-art surveillance equipment as if you were Q. Extracting a pound of flesh has only become more fun with all of these doodads. And a freebie comes with your purchases: the anonymity factor. Doing things like sending unidentified text messages to someone's cell phone is reminiscent of the good ol' days of prank calling, when you could get away with it since caller ID was only a futuristic concept and *69 only a sex position.

Hooking Up Online

One woman found out about her partner's infidelity when he moronically forgot to sign out of his e-mail. She quickly discovered that he had sought prostitutes and hooked up with other women via the Internet. She decided to gather as much evidence as she could, and then posed as someone he'd definitely want to chat with. He fell for it hook, line, and sinker, e-mailing her thirty times in one day. Forget "You've Got Mail!" You've got questions to answer!

There are countless ways to make a keyboard and the satellite your own personal weapons of choice when you want to exact revenge. And as long as it's safe and legal, Nick James of getrevengeonyourex.com believed that people feel empowered once they've actually done something about getting revenge, that "you are no longer a victim just sitting there. And it's this sense of control that revenge gives you that helps you to move on." He also believed that revenge should follow one rule: Be funny. It's a good reminder that revenge shouldn't be taken too seriously, and besides, isn't laughter the best medicine for a broken heart? "Laughing classes" (and even documentary films like *The Laughing Club of India*) are popping up around the world as a means of de-stressing and taking one's mind off things like your lying, cheating bastard. Although this book isn't a class or an instruction manual, hopefully you'll be belly-full with blissful aches from laughing at how others have utilized today's technology.

Revenge Sex

Urban Dictionary defines "revenge sex" as "Sex that occurs as a direct result of a nymphomaniacal need for sex after a fight or other type of malicious behavior. Also linked to makeup sex, makeup sex as a result of a preplanned fight or argument, and angry sex." Sarah Silverman did a parody of this concept by making a music video in which she pretended she was cheating on her then-boyfriend, TV host Jimmy Kimmel, with actor Matt Damon. It busted out as a huge favorite on YouTube. Kimmel retaliated by pretending he was cheating on her with actor Ben Affleck. Hilarity ensued, with fantastic cameos . . . but revenge sex unfortunately is not always this funny.

One example of what James did as part of his online revenge service was place an ad in a gay online magazine in the classifieds' "looking for a roommate" section. He said this was a tactic that worked best when the man was very good-looking—although he didn't reveal names (only their photos). James said he did this once to a famous UK TV celebrity and "the effect was brilliant and even made the tabloid press."

Techno-venge

Here are some actions and reactions to the advancement of extramarital romance and technology:

MOUSE ATTACK

Hunting is big in China. Internet hunting of adulterers, that is. Web users have been taking advantage of the wild,

wild cyberspace, teaming up with hordes of furious mouse clickers to track down, investigate, and punish cheaters while remaining anonymous. And this is all done in the name of morality.

An example: One husband ("Freezing Blade") thought his wife ("Quiet Moon") was humping a college student ("Bronze Mustache"). So Freezing Blade posted the real name of Bronze Mustache on a hip online video game, "World of Warcraft," saying this guy was engaging in some serious extracurricular activity with his wife. The response was overwhelming, turning into China's own contemporary Salem witch hunt, with online mobs wanting to punish Bronze Mustache for his behavior and lack of morals. Soon enough, Bronze's phone number and address were also made public, and erasing information from cyberspace is as easy as rubbing out indelible ink. According to Howard French's article in *The New York Times* "Mob Rule on China's Internet: The Keyboard As Weapon," the game put up a manifesto that stated: "We call on every company, every establishment, every office, school, hospital, shopping mall, and public street to reject him. Don't accept him, don't admit him, don't identify with him until he makes a satisfying and convincing repentance." As a result, Bronze Mustache was forced to drop out of school and go into hiding with his family inside their home. In desperation, he put together a short video in which he denied the affair. Even the husband, who started all this but recognized that things had gotten a little out of hand, supposedly asked for people to call off the attacks.

DADDY'S LITTLE GIRL

The Internet can also be a place to deal with family affairs—literally. Again in China, an only daughter, who was fiercely devoted to her mother, decided to punish her unfaithful father. She created an "anti-mistress" Web site, where she detailed her papa's bad-boy behavior, reminiscing about their family life that once was, even posting petitions for him to stop his cheating ways.

SHUT OFF FROM THE WORLD

Technology has also given us the freedom to be anywhere at any time and reachable without having to reveal our true location. There's a story (probably an urban legend) about a man who worked at the World Trade Center in New York City who took full advantage of the cord-free nature of his cell phone. On the tragic day of 9/11, his wife was frantically calling him, trying to reach him. When she finally got through, she immediately asked, "Are you okay?" The man said, "Sure." Then she asked, "Where are you?" He answered, "At the office, at my desk, why?" He had been having a morning session with his lover in a hotel room with closed curtains and had turned off his cell phone and made sure not to have any other outside distractions. He had no idea about the horrors that had been going on in downtown Manhattan that morning or that his entire office building no longer existed.

Uptown, Downturn

E-mails are how Christie Brinkley reportedly confirmed that her spouse, Peter Cook, was getting it on with a local teenager, after the teen's stepfather told her about it. But during the divorce proceedings, Cook's lawyer tried to turn the tables by blaming Brinkley (who has been married four times): "Your honor, we're here because of the self-indulgent wrath of a woman scorned." Whatever the case, even supermodels are not immune to cheating hubbies.

PUBLIC CYBER FEUD

When former Playmate Shanna Moakler and former Blink-182 drummer Travis Barker were going through their divorce, they no longer had their reality TV show, *Meet the Barkers,* to duke it out on. So they found a new public venue on MySpace (well, who would want to keep this stuff private if it could raise his or her celebrity status?). Both of them blogged about each other and carried on their feud in cyberspace for all the world to see. But perhaps their MySpace sites didn't get as many hits as they had hoped since the latest news reports that they're back together.

Unusual Freelance Gigs

One (married) woman was getting annoyed at her online lover's wife for getting in the way of their relationship and decided to have her knocked off. She reached out through Craigslist, offering $5,000 to whoever would complete her mission. The job was under the heading of "freelance." The cops came around to arrest her before someone picked up the gig.

HEART PAINS

"Kate" described how she and her husband, "Joe," had been best friends and partners for many years. They decided to get married, but it was only a year before she discovered that he was sleeping with his coworker. How did she find out? She happened upon their secret e-mail account just as she and Joe were relocating to a different city. But when Kate confronted Joe, he explained that the coworker had an innocent crush on him. So Kate let things slide, especially since they were about to have a brand-new start in a new city. But after one month, she realized that Joe was still in touch with the woman. When she confronted Joe again, he not only admitted to the affair but he became very open about it, texting, e-mailing, and calling the woman right in front of Kate.

Kate was in a sticky situation because she was pregnant with their first child. She had a serious decision to make about her future. Would she be better off as a single parent? Joe wasn't making things easy for her: He continued the relationship with his coworker and even suggested that Kate get an abortion. So Kate mustered up all the courage she could and decided she was going to become a single mom, packed up, and moved out, going right back to the city they had recently moved from.

Kate then mailed her wedding band and a letter of explanation to Joe's girlfriend's devoutly religious parents. She warned them about Joe, saying he was a liar and that he was dumping his pregnant wife to be with their daughter.

The girlfriend's father had to be admitted to the hospital with chest pains after he read the letter.

Putting the Digital Revolution in Your Corner

Whether he was unfaithful or simply treating you like dirt, there are many revolutionary and groundbreaking ways to get back at someone who just broke your heart, all the while keeping your finger on the pulse of the Digital Age. Even PIs agree that technology has made everything easier in regards to investigations or uncovering steamy love affairs. According to Gary DeFinis, the private investigator I spoke with, gone are the days of the gumshoes when a lot of time was spent knocking on doors. Today, at the touch of a button, you have all the information you need in an instant. And being able to understand and utilize that information once you have it is key.

real life (they held a ceremony online). But after she caught Pollard hanging out affectionately with an online hostess, or virtual prostitute, played by another woman, she called "game over" for their cyber and real-life marriage.

THE DANGERS

Before we delve into cyber tactics, it's probably wise to keep a few things in mind in order to keep you from ending up in the slammer. While the Internet is appealing because it allows a certain anonymity, like the other revenge tactics discussed in this book, it can also cause serious damage to the target and to you.

There is the risk of crossing the line into "cyber stalking," which can truly be frightening. Men and women are both guilty of this. They're livid about being rejected and do things like post details of their exes on sexually explicit Web sites, send endless e-mails, and fabricate text messages. For example, one jilted husband, who had reportedly been abusive to his wife, was so angry that she left him that he posted her details on his Web site, a mail-order cross-dressing service for men. The phone calls and e-mails she got from men interested in she-males, which he represented her as, freaked her out. In an article in the UK's *Guardian*, an expert on stalking, Dr. Lorraine Sheridan, said that half of all stalker victims are now under attack courtesy of the Internet. And the Internet is not only making things easier for stalkers, but it also seems to be encouraging them with the flood of new Web sites and online communities focused on how to pinpoint someone's whereabouts. There currently is no restraining order that can remedy the too-close-for-comfort proximity that the Internet provides someone.

Cyber Stalker

Jeffrey Evans of the UK snapped topless photos of his girl-friend and put them to use after they split. He advertised her as a prostitute in as many bar bathrooms as possible, and even put an ad in a porn magazine. In a text message to his ex, he wrote, "This is just a taste—there are some really horrible things to come."

The police ended up finding other ads he was going to place that said things like his ex was willing to exchange sex for cash so that she could pay her mortgage. Evans was sentenced to eight months in prison. The reason the ex had dumped him in the first place? He couldn't get it together to find a job.

Stalking on the Internet can come in other forms, such as cyber bullying, a staple in any cyber recess yard. It's simple: If you don't like somebody, you go to all of the online forums with which you know that person is associated and smear his or her name through the mud. No more writing "Johnny has a small penis" on lockers. Now, kids can post even meaner things on Web sites and message boards for all the world to see.

Steve Yoshimura of the University of Montana considers cyber bullying a revenge tactic as well. "It's not just people overpowering other people," he says of this method of harassment, which is mostly associated with high-school kids but can easily extend to any age group. "It's people who feel offended by somebody [and are] targeting that person for punishment." School fights in hallways are a pleasant dream when compared to the nightmare that slants and humiliation can pose when posted online for everyone to read and see, and to potentially haunt you the rest of your life.

Most laws against those using the Internet to harass or victimize people are just plain vague when it comes to what is and isn't illegal on the wild, wild Web. However, with the creation of departments such as the Computer Crime & Intellectual Property Section (or cybercrime) in the U.S. Department of Justice, more policy makers are trying to change that and up the punishment—rightly so, since this kind of "play" has resulted in serious, even deadly, consequences. For example, Representative Mark Green (R-Wisconsin) attempted to enact the Personal Pictures Protection Act, which would "amend existing law to prohibit the publication of sexually explicit photos of people on the Internet without their prior consent." In 2006, President Bush signed into law, through Section 113 of the Violence Against Women Act, that anyone sending e-mails or making Web postings "without disclosing his identity and with intent to annoy, abuse, threaten, or harass any person" is committing a federal crime. This ignited fierce debate, since the word *annoy* can be interpreted in many ways. And one way can be when you're getting back at your ex.

So, as I've cautioned throughout, let's keep things legal, and please, do not become obsessive. Don't spend all of your time stalking your computer and checking your "Google alerts," hoping something will pop up that will give you a clue as to his whereabouts. Don't become addicted to the Refresh button just to make sure that in those last 10.5 seconds you didn't miss something popping up on the Web about him. It's not worth your time, eyesight, or sanity.

That said, you're on your own, and you're going to find

and use the resources you need to get back at him so that you can even the emotional playing field. And with a little IT support, you will be able to do just that.

Down and Dirty Poetry

One UK woman not only dumped her boyfriend, she also stole a bunch of his cash. Unable to retrieve the money, he decided to find a creative outlet for his broke state of mind. He wrote a series of poems about her and created a Web site where he posted all of them. But the ex didn't find the site quite as poetic, so she complained to the police, who evidently found the poems to be "pretty good."

The Power of the Written Word

Did you save all the e-mails he sent you as mementos, so that you two could read them together during one of your future anniversaries? Before you hit Delete All, contemplate a different use for them now. One person showed off her literary skills and made a composition of them, plucking different lines from this e-mail and that e-mail, adding a few of her own, and posting them as *his* brilliant words. Maybe this made him look like a jackass, maybe this empowered her.

Blogs are also a place where people have taken advantage of composing "his" words, updating it with their thoughts, theories, and thrashings. Never underestimate the keyboard's might. Dr. Susan Boon of the University of Calgary said she knew of a woman who broke up with her boyfriend and then wrote a blog about how much she liked her ex-boyfriend—the ex *before* the ex!

Another woman—mentioned by Boon—got into her ex's e-mail account and sent really dumb questions to his professor. The professor quickly responded that the man clearly needed extra help and he better come as soon as possible in order not to fail his class!

The Blog

With the increase in blogs sprouting up all over the Internet comes the increase in subject matter. So it's inevitable that some of these blogs are about broken relationships, and they're used as a means to get revenge. For example, "Ex-Girlfriend's Revenge" is a popular blog written by a British woman who decided to get back at all her exes by writing about all of their inadequacies—with the "main" ex being nicknamed The Beast.

When you're living together, it's hard to keep things secret. If anything, you've both let your guard down at some point and shared just about everything. That includes passwords to your computers and online accounts. One fantasy, clearly off-limits: Some people have even gone to the extreme of deleting an entire hard drive. Instead maybe just tell him to pack up and back up when you dump his cheating ass.

While scouring his old e-mails for other evidence of his illicit affairs or impending desire to sever your relationship, why not have some fun? Post a classified ad for a cheating husband or a lowlife, loser of a husband on auction sites like eBay. Going once, going twice . . . See how much he's really worth!

The Power of the Net

Make sure he gets plenty of advertisements for Viagra or penile enlargement operations (*no* guy ever thinks he's big enough!) sent to his e-mail account, as if someone's trying to give him a hint.

of 'The Tart's' knickers." She also gave a detailed account of how she discovered the infidelity. Next on her list of items to sell was her husband's motorcycle—for about $1!

Hate all those annoying CALL BACK and FREE GIVEAWAY signs flashing on your screen? Finally, a reason to click on them: enter his name, phone number, and e-mail. They'll inundate him with calls and spam e-mails immediately, and then keep calling and spamming him. In addition, his e-mail account will be flooded with messages touting "debt solution," "free PlayStations," and "horny teens who need your manhood."

Spelling It Out

According to Raymond DiGiuseppe of St. John's University, one scorned woman took out an ad on Craigslist that read, "Looking for a hunk of a guy? For great gay sex, call me at . . ." and left her husband's cell-phone number—by literally spelling out all the numbers. Sure enough, he was barraged with calls.

The Podcast

Talk about voicing vengeance. DivorcingDaze (www.divorcingdaze.com) resulted from one woman's discovery of her husband cheating on her with his boss. She and her friend would have a glass of wine and talk (or rather, vent) about various subjects, including their divorce journeys and lousy, cheating exes. They taped their conversations and uploaded them onto the site. But her ex not only found it *not* to be funny, he sued her. She got off with a little ol' thing called the First Amendment on her side and more hits than ever on her site. She claimed the site wasn't meant as retribution.

Hijacking can happen on MySpace and Facebook pages. Could you imagine if a vengeful ex changed his name to "Pathological Liar" and his profession to "Cheating Scumbag." Worse yet, if she changed his password so that he got stuck . . . at least long enough to break a sweat? Funny to think about—but not funny to do.

Wicked Wiki

Jimmy Wales, cofounder of the online encyclopedia Wikipedia, met Fox TV's commentator Rachel Marsden when she started to have issues with her bio on the site. Editing brought on some hot and heavy exclamation points between the two, until Wales decided to dump Marsden. Thing was, he didn't do it in person but rather, in his entry on Wikipedia. In return, Marsden forwarded their steamy IMs and her breakup letter (in which she called him a "sleazebag") to the site, and also sold clothing he left behind in her apartment on eBay.

GotVoice is a free program that retrieves voice messages from an existing phone and sends them directly to your e-mail in-box, in text mode. You get the lowdown on who's calling him and leaving him voice mail. It's not hard to believe someone has probably taken advantage of that and erased all "his" messages without him even knowing about it.

Dicking Around on E-Mail

One woman, suspicious that her husband was cheating on her, sent an e-mail from his account to his entire address book, titled "Time to Fess Up!" that read, "I, Paul Owen Evans, am a sniveling, cheating, lying, arrogant little piece of shit. No, that's not right—I'm worse than that: I'm a despicable, deceitful, dodgy DICKHEAD who doesn't reserve this attitude just for his wife. Oh yes, one more thing—I've got an extremely small penis that couldn't excite a woman's nostril, let alone anything else. Thus endeth my confession. Regards, Paul Evans."

Is he a gamer? Does he have the latest Xbox 360, Nintendo Wii, or PlayStation? Of course, you could get a fortune by putting those items up on eBay, and buy yourself some Manolo Blahniks with his video game accessories. But don't stop your fantasizing there. Does he spend hours collecting armor and weapons and cars and levels? So that means he fantasizes too. Imagine what it'd be like if you "accidentally" erased all of the memory from his console.

One Japanese woman playing an online virtual video game called Maple Story was so angry that her "online husband" dumped her in the virtual world, she busted into his account and killed off his video game character, or avatar. She was then busted for illegally breaking into a computer and messing with electronic data. She is quoted as saying: "I was suddenly divorced, without a word of warning. That made me so angry."

A Different Kind of Passion

One woman had enough of her husband's obsession with sports memorabilia. After he had spent their entire life savings on baseball cards and other crap—er...paraphernalia—she decided to put her foot down. What made her finally take a stance? He took her car and the last of their money to go to Cooperstown, home of the Baseball Hall of Fame. So when he returned, she welcomed him back with divorce papers. Then, she won all of his collections in the divorce and sold them on eBay, with a headline that read "Divorced and Finally Getting Her Due."

A Picture Is Worth a Thousand Words

Have a leftover collection of naked photos you took of him one drunken night? Or of him dressing up in your lingerie? Wait! Don't burn 'em! You never know when they can come in handy. Some people have posted them online . . . people are always willing to buy photos for a good cause.

Go to HotorNot.com and put the worst mug shot you can find of him up there. Then spam the link to friends and family for their enjoyment.

Bargain Poses

Be careful what you pose for. One husband put two hundred sexy photos of his cheating ex on eBay. Within twenty-four

(continued)

hours, they were sold. Another man sent a naked photo of his cheating girlfriend to everyone in her e-mail address book. It was one of the photos they took earlier on in their relationship in order to spice things up.

One stripper sold photos of Oscar De La Hoya, made-up and decked out in female undies, fishnets, and heels. She then proceeded to sue the famous boxer when he claimed the photographs were doctored. She dropped the suit when experts said they were.

The Techno Art of Revenge

French Artist Sophie Calle decided to get creative on her ex who broke up with her via e-mail. He had typed her a pathetic letter stating it was best they end things since he'd realized he had a wandering eye for other ladies and didn't want to cheat on her. He claimed it was for her own good that they end their relationship.

Calle didn't resort to tears after the breakup; instead, she created an art piece titled *Take Care of Yourself* (his closing words in the e-mail) that filled the French pavilion at the Venice Biennale. She asked more than a hundred women to read and interpret the e-mail, according to their profession. Some highlights: Calle had a judge judge it; she had a forensic psychiatrist analyze the text (her opinion was that it had been written by "a true, twisted manipulator, psychologically dangerous and/or a great writer. To be avoided, categorically"), and she had the letter translated into various languages, Morse code, shorthand, and so on. She had it turned into a crossword puzzle; she had actresses—such as Jeanne Moreau, Miranda Richardson, and Vanessa Redgrave—a clown, and a puppeteer read the letter on video and make their own remarks; she had dancers choreograph an interpretative dance to it. On top of all this, she had blown-up versions of the e-mail on the walls, along with videos of herself sitting in a shrink's office with the e-mail in the empty chair beside her. She made sure that the exhibit had tons of humor and artistic quality and provided visitors an opportunity to laugh at her ex's arrogance.

Although she claims her mission in creating this piece of artwork was actually not revenge, it's hard to imagine it as anything else.

Is he into meeting new people online? Why not get a friend to pretend she's someone else, a hot Russian or whatever he's into. She can start a relationship with him online, send him photos (not of her but of a magazine model), and get him to send her photos of himself—preferably, showing off his privates. Some men have let themselves get exposed in this way. Then let the pictures run wild online, hitting up everyone he knows and any girl who lives within a twenty-five-square-mile radius of him.

VIDEO-VENGE

Speaking of images, YouTube is where you should surf next. There are already many videos that have been edited, altered, or positioned in a way to compromise "his" manhood, size, and dignity.

One filmmaker, Colin Trevorrow, decided that one way to discuss how bitter male/female relations have become was through a short film about—what else?—revenge.

The film, *Home Base*, was featured on YouTube and various other sites. The plot: A guy is dumped by his girlfriend for another guy. What does the dumped character say after hearing the news? "It makes things clear, because now I know exactly what I have to do. Now I'm gonna fuck your mom." And that's precisely what he does. He wines and dines the ex-girlfriend's mother and eventually gets her into the sack with him.

While this hilarious little movie was fabricated, it does raise the question: Why not think about pushing your directing and/or producing skills forward and making your own film about your experience with the schmuck? Maybe the story is how your ex dumped you and how you got back at him. There are even video-sharing sites that will pay you if you get enough hits. Bonus!

Divorce, YouTube-Style

Tricia Walsh-Smith catapulted her impending divorce to a whole new level—and to a whole new audience—when she decided to use YouTube as her platform to discuss the down and dirty secrets of her marriage to mega Broadway wheeler-dealer (aka president of the Schubert Organization) Philip Smith.

The forty-nine-year-old, UK-born Walsh-Smith ranted and raved that Smith, who dumped her, was trying to kick her out of their Upper East Side apartment and wanted to leave her with basically nothing (she apparently signed a lousy prenup). So she decided to let the world peek into the world of their marriage—and more than two million people did. Apparently, they had no sex (he's seventy-four), and she even called Smith's office (on camera) and let his secretary in on their sex life, saying that despite her husband's high blood pressure's not allowing him to have sex, she had found Viagra, condoms, and porn among his things. She also pointed out the "evil" members of Smith's family, photographed in their wedding album. And she of course lamented the career she once had (she wrote a produced play and had done some acting—although some may argue that this YouTube was her most memorable performance). Her YouTube appearance backfired, since the judge decided that her hubby had been treated cruelly and inhumanely, and therefore granted a divorce. Smith also didn't have to give her anything more than what was in their prenup—$750,000—and thirty days to vacate his apartment.

One woman was furious when her boyfriend left her, so she decided to make him a star by putting an intimate video of them online. To make sure it got the most possible hits, she sent messages to all the guests at his twenty-first birthday party so that they'd watch!

And one guy secretly filmed himself having sex with his girlfriend. When she dumped him, he used today's computer advancements to get his revenge—by making his own DVDs of the sex tapes and placing them, along with her contact details, on the windshields of cars. If he had any hopes of producing more films like that, they were dashed when he was charged with using a computer to "carry out the production of obscene exhibition," plus a few other offenses. When it comes to your own situation, tread lightly when using homemade porn, just like any other revenge tactic.

Why Do People Still Agree to Homemade Sex Tapes?

"Tim" revealed how he usually, after a few weeks of dating someone, videotapes the sex they have—with the girl's consent. He then saves the video on his computer.

But one *forgetful* girl cheated on him, and she ended up paying big-time for that mistake. Tim built a Web site around their sex video, decorated it with her photos, and sent the site's link to everyone he knew—and people she knew. He even went to the extent of taking out an ad in a porn magazine to promote the video.

RAMming Your Point Home

Although there are countless ways to get back at your ex online, several Web sites have specifically carved out a niche that can play into the hands of scorned women (and men). Here are just a few. (Please note that there's no guarantee these sites will still be up when you read this book since these sites can be just as capricious as your ex!)

Getrevengeonyourex.com. Here's a site devoted to helping scorned lovers get even with their exes. It was started by Nick James, who sadly passed away in 2008 and has already been quoted in this book. He was cheated on and decided to get revenge by doing things like putting dog shit on the underside of his ex-wife's boyfriend's car door handles. "It is incredibly difficult to describe the sense of relief I got from actually doing something tangible," said James. "In my mind, I was no longer just sitting there drowning in my sorrows—I was actually doing something." He pulled a few more pranks and said that he started to feel better and better about doing these things—childish or not—and people around him noticed his good mood. When he told them about his plots and plans, they in turn asked for his help to get back at their own exes. So James decided that everything in the world should have a Web site, even revenge.

On his public revenge site, he would post humiliating photos of your ex, send him or her insulting text messages, or mail embarrassing postcards—and keep everything anonymous. He would even go so far as to make a personal phone call to an ex with a nasty message of your choice. "The thing with getting revenge is not so that you can forget what your ex has done and move on," James explained. "It's about regaining control of your emotions." When I was in touch with James, he was happily married and felt great about being able to help others get through tough breakups. "I get a kick out of knowing the bad guys are getting their comeuppance—each time I send a package or make a call, I know that the recipient is no longer in control and that's exactly how my clients feel, so in some way, I'm helping to right a wrong."

With an average of six hundred to a thousand hits a day (85 percent of his clients are women), his site was—and still is—kind of like the A-Team except more like the R-Team. "Even if people don't buy anything, the site allows them to at least fantasize about getting revenge and they also realize that they are not alone," said James. "There is a real solidarity among the members."

RevengeLady.com. As she puts it: "Revenge Lady gives advice on using the ancient art of revenge to bring humor and happiness back to your life. Come rediscover this traditional code of honor. Revenge advice. It's justice, plain and simple." Her site is filled with stories and offers services such as a "Get Lost" letter which she'll write *and* send out for you. If ancient Mesopotamia had great revenge tactics, she'll know.

RevengeGuy.com. Want a guy's perspective on how to get revenge on your ex? Here it is! While this site is for both men and women, you can find pretty much whatever you need, from breakup lines to vengeance ideas to T-shirts with attitudes. The revenge guy's got balls.

Soyouvebeendumped.com. This is not entirely a revenge site, since its focus is to offer support and advice during a breakup, but it does present the chance to write an article—a "name and shame piece," as it's called on the site—so you can not only feel as if you've served up some just desert, but you're getting paid to do it as well. (Note: This site is UK based and only offers this in UK newspapers.) Plus, SYBD gives tips on how to get over being dumped, and a titillating list of best "breakup lines" that will surely bring on a giggle, whether or not it's a line that's been used on you before!

DontDateHimGirl.com. Created by Tasha Joseph in Miami, the site allows users to post pictures and "cheat sheets" of alleged philandering men for all to see. It's free and available 24/7.

ThePayback.com. This "don't get mad . . . get even!" site is devoted to a variety of the different types of revenge you can exact (from planting dead fish to sending anonymous e-mails regarding body odor), catered to the type of person you are getting back at. It's like a build-your-own-revenge workshop.

MakeHimPay.net. The site states, "Don't waste time crying over your loser or ex-boyfriend ex-husband when you can be laughing at him instead." It was founded by a woman who found out her boyfriend was cheating, and she wasn't going to take it lying down. So on top of her own revenge tactics, such as forwarding all calls made to his phone number to a gay porn line, she decided that there was no better way to move on than to help others bust their significant others—and treat them to a down and dirty dose of revenge.

WomanSavers.com. This site has a message board where women can rant about the lying, cheating men who have abused, lied, or deceived them. There is a "Rate-a-Guy" form, where you enter the name of the guy in question and write up what you can about him to make sure no one else ends up with such a jerk. And if you want to find out if he's on the site, you can click "Search-a-Guy." To keep things fair and balanced, the site does offer a message board where men can post their own comments, even relating their own stories of being cheated on!

Avengers Den (www.avengersden.com). In addition to revenge ideas and resources, this site offers discussions and photos of exes, and some juicy, true tales of revenge.

The Ashley Madison Agency (www.ashleymadison.com). Do you think having your own affair is the way to get revenge? If you're convinced it is, this site can probably help. The site claims that monogamy has never worked anyway, so why not have a place for cheating spouses to go and start up more affairs? Beware: This site may begin or continue one long and vicious cycle.

Revenge Unlimited (www.revengeunlimited.com). Basically, this is an online shop full of fun—and sometimes silly—gadgets and pranks to get back at him. Load up on "small pecker condoms" and "revenge toilet paper" and you're set to go! Kind of like gearing up for another bachelorette party.

Ex-Boyfriend Jewelry (www.exboyfriendjewelry.com). Give emotional baggage new meaning by making some bucks off of it! Women can dust off all the old pieces of jewelry from their exes and put them up for sale online, along with comments, sagas, and venting.

There are the "dirtier" sites such as Revenge World (www. revengeworld.com) that offer revenge, coupled with a whole lot of . . . naked coupling (whether it's a naked photo of an ex or all the porn ads that lace the side panels of the site). And www.revengecrabs.com—the revenge that keeps on giving.

To find out what other kinds of pranks you can do, or to get some sites to pull some pranks for you, go to www .PrankPlace.com or www.pranksite.com or www.Prank Space.com or www.StrangeReports.com or www.computer pranks.com or www.free-revenge-ideas.com or www.college humor.com or . . . okay, enough for now.

There are still other services out there that you can exploit. Check these out:

Go to a popular Web site for chatting and erotic stories, such as Literotica (www.literotica.com). After registering under a fake name, write in depth about how you love to talk nasty over the phone and sign off as your ex, with his real name and all his phone numbers (including the front desk at his job). Or submit a short story "he" wrote to their contest and see what response it gets! Make sure you follow up with an enthusiastic e-mail to all of his friends, family, and colleagues to check out the new scribe.

DeadRoses.com will ship roses to your ex with nasty notes like "Roses are red, violets are blue. These roses are dead and I wish you were too!" Maya Angelou would be so proud.

RelationShipOver.com will send a wide variety of items, such as a revenge basket, filled with items that have themes. For example, a "small penis basket" or "douche bag basket"; not-so-nice candy (such as a cookie tin filled with what looks and smells like dog crap!); or a personalized breakup video. Any vengeful spirit would feel as if she scored her very own treasure chest!

On the flip side of the coin: Are you the victim of having your reputation smudged all over the Internet? There's a way to restore that now, with the help of a new company called Reputation Defender (www.reputationdefender.com). You can get all sorts of packages—from just finding out what's said about you online to getting sites to remove negative content about you to changing the placement of search results. A lot of nasty bytes can float into cyberspace and you may have to do some damage control to land back on your feet in the real world.

So kick back with your laptop and click and hang ten in cyber land. As enticing as it is to peer into other people's sites and blogs, and to stir up a little e-venge of your own, be cognizant of pointing and clicking way too much—like, take notice if you're getting carpal tunnel syndrome from overusing your mouse or your vision has become blurry from staring at the screen: It may mean you need to take a breather, like reading the rest of this book.

Chapter 8

WHEN VENGEANCE BACKFIRES

You've done it! You've gotten your revenge. Your husband's BMW has sugar in the fuel line, his e-mail signature now has an amputee porn site added to it, his mother is watching a tape made during a fraternity house threesome (yes, the swords crossed). You feel good about yourself. You're looking forward to a bright future, whether with prince charming or (but hopefully not) cell block D. You were right about the cheating bastard and you've now kicked back on the sofa with a freshly baked (but not laced) batch of brownies, ready to watch a movie and carry on with your life.

> Living a life of revenge often backfires. It's all negativity and we often hurt innocent people; extremely messy.— Shakespeare, *Hamlet*

When Things Bite Back

But your moral and ethical angel stands on your shoulder. Should you have done this? Will this backfire on you? Does karma really burn? And, if so, does it cause second- or third-degree burns?

Burned

One pissed-off guy got drunk and convinced a friend to burn his ex-girlfriend's bed (and other areas of her home) as payback for her coupling with another guy. Lucky for the ex-girlfriend, she was out of town. And the two men got busted and were found guilty of arson. They spent a few years in jail each.

What might have happened because of your revenge? The clothes,
which you meticulously unstitched,
fell off your husband in the middle of
the bar. It was embarrassing. It was
supposed to be. But not to the blond
bartender who came to his aid. They might
be an item now because of it.

Here are some tales about the ways that revenge can backfire . . . and some lessons to be learned.

Written Off

If you decided to use your literacy skills as your weapon for
revenge, make sure you know how powerful the person is that
you're writing about. One of Jennifer Lopez's exes, Ojani Noa,
tried to write a tell-all book about his marriage to J-Lo, but
J-Lo put the brakes on that project quickly by unleashing her
lawyers on him. In addition, Noa had to pay up for violating a
signed confidentiality agreement.

HIDE AND LEAK

Be careful where you decide to spy on your hubby. One
Pittsburgh woman hid under her husband's SUV to survey a
house in which she assumed her husband was playing peek-
a-boo with his zipper. But as happens on many a stakeout,
she fell asleep, only to be awoken by a strange person letting
the air out of the car's tires, crushing her. She screamed until
a nearby worker found her under the car and managed to get
her out, safe and sound. After that, it'd be surprising if the
marriage didn't lose all its air as well. But the oddest part

about it was that no one appears to know who let the air out of those tires, or why.

Computer Skills

A Connecticut woman, Pilar Stofega, was hell-bent on breaking up her ex's marriage and decided one way to do that was to create fake profiles of the "new wife" on various adult Web sites. When the wife started getting calls from strangers (Stofega posted the wife's phone numbers and her high-school yearbook photo on the site), her husband did a little investigation of his own and tracked down his ex from years ago. She was slapped with a second-degree harassment and breach of peace charge, and was released on a $2,500 bond.

SPACED-OUT RELATIONSHIPS

Astronaut Lisa Nowak, who once flew in the space shuttle Discovery, appeared to have lost her marbles when she found out that her boyfriend, fellow shuttle pilot Bill Oefelein, was turning the International Space Station into the International Love Station: He was discovering another female ass-troid belt and e-mailing this cosmo-chick, Colleen Shipman. Nowak took matters into her own hands when she broke into his computer to gather Shipman's flight details and then made an infamous drive from Houston to Orlando to confront her. Mind you, Nowak was a married woman of nineteen years, and a mother of three. It was even rumored that she supposedly prepped for the trip by strapping on a diaper in order to avoid stops, and she made sure she had everything she needed in her suitcase: knife, BB gun (she was planning to sting someone to death), steel mallet, garbage bags, wig, trench coat, and pepper spray. It's party time!

Nowak allegedly approached Shipman at her car wearing the wig and trench coat, then squirted her with pepper spray before Shipman fled as fast as she could. Nowak was eventually charged with attempted kidnapping and burglary with assault. Her saga was astronomical news. Not only was it a love triangle involving three NASA astronauts, who were supposed to have been thoroughly vetted psychologically, it was also an extraordinary tale of one woman's almost insane determination to get rid of her competition.

Personally, I find the concept of revenge hard to justify. I think that revenge always comes back, like a boomerang, and hurts you just as hard as you tried to hurt the other person.

I remember one summer, when my friends and I were fifteen or sixteen years old and hitchhiking around Poland. We were on some country back road, hoping a car would stop to pick us up, but no one would stop for hours. Finally, a huge truck approached with some empty passenger seats. Hopeful, we waved to the driver. Not only did he not even slow down, he also made a sign with his finger, as if we were crazy, followed by some other obscene gestures. In revenge, I drew my cheeks in and crossed my arms under my chin to symbolize a skull and bones, as if I were cursing him. A half hour later, we finally got a ride. A few kilometers down the road, we passed the same truck, flipped over. Next to it was the dead body of the driver. This incident sent a chill down my spine, as I felt somewhat responsible for his demise.

Many years later, I reflexively made that same gesture, angry with a producer who had ruined one of my movies. Soon after our confrontation, the young woman died from cancer. This experience completely erased any thoughts of revenge from my mind forever.

When the men in my life have hurt or betrayed me, I've always tried to understand them and, instead of exacting revenge, feel some kind of cold empathy toward their actions. While preparing to direct my movie *Washington Square,* I watched William Wyler's version, which was very popular in the United States. The leitmotif of his adaptation was revenge, which seems to be very deeply rooted in American mentality and favored by audiences here. But this take on Henry James's story seemed incongruous with his philosophy, at least the way I understood it, and I did everything possible to avoid that direction. There's an old proverb that calls revenge God's delight. To me, though, revenge is nothing more than poison.—filmmaker Agnieszka Holland

UNFORTUNATE FEEDBACK

A husband had a radio station call his wife to pull a prank on her. The radio announcer pretended to be a manager calling from her husband's work. He told the wife that he unfortunately had to let the husband go. The wife was upset and confused by the news and complained about the bad timing because they just had a baby. She said her husband had always "been so loyal" to the company. But then the radio announcer revealed why they had to fire him: "We caught him doing his secretary on his office desk." Needless to say, the wife wasn't so happy to hear this. She lashed out at the DJ who was orchestrating this practical joke, and said, "Now, I don't feel so bad about fucking his brother!" The husband had been on the line the whole time, listening to every word . . . and to their relationship combust.

WIFE PORN

One Malaysian businessman tried to get back at his estranged wife by posting lewd pictures of her online and offering her up for sex. The mother of his children started to get calls from interested parties all over the world. But the man forgot his own country's laws: Under Malaysia's Computer

Crimes Act, he now faces up to ten years in jail or a maximum fine of approximately $39,000.

Shakespeare had a few choice words about revenge in his *Henry VIII*: Heat not a furnace for your foe / That it do singe yourself.

KINGS WILL BE KINGS

According to legend, a Roman king of Judea, King Herod, killed his wife, Mariamne, after his sister, Salome, accused her of an assassination plot. Thing was, Salome was lying. The king supposedly grieved by embalming Mariamne and having sex with her corpse for years.

One Tubful of Revenge

The late Lisa "Left Eye" Lopes of TLC used to date Andre Rison, a wide receiver on the Atlanta Falcons, and they had one fiery relationship. During one of their countless fights, Lisa made a bonfire in the bathtub of all of Andre's cute little teddy bears. (Teddy bears?) Later, after yet another fight, Lisa set another bathtub on fire, which melted since it was fiberglass and torched Andre's house. She was sentenced to five years probation and a $10,000 fine. And after all that, they still got engaged!

GAMING WIPE

One Japanese man picked the wrong day to break up with his girlfriend. She busted into his online game account, Lineage, using his password and user name, and deleted his data, which he had accumulated over many hours devoted to the game. But there's a lesson to be learned here: She was caught and reported for "violating a law banning illegal access."

PLACING CALLS ONLINE

Don't let those late-night calls come back to haunt you. One Dallas man put up a Web site called psychoexgirlfriend .com and posted about fifty crazy voice-mail messages from his ex on it. The site got millions of hits. 'Nuff said.

The Awkward Watercooler

"Zack" recounted his story while he was in the midst of exacting his revenge. He had met a woman, "Melanie," at work who was a divorced, single mother. They became friendly, spoke occasionally, sent each other e-mails, and even had shy watercooler chats. However, they were never intimate; they never even kissed. He was smitten, though, and decided to write her a love letter. To his surprise, she not only didn't respond to the letter, but she also stopped communicating with him altogether. When he finally ran into her at work, she suggested that they keep things casual and just be friends. Shamed, he apologized for coming on too strong.

Soon after, Zack was called into his manager's office for a little chat. Turns out, Melanie had reported him for harassing her. He was told he could no longer communicate with her, and he had to participate in a sexual harassment course. Zack was scared shitless upon hearing the news and eventually found a lawyer to write a rebuttal memo.

(continued)

Zack snapped out of the initial shock of all this, and went from hurt and confused to just plain pissed. He proceeded to delve down a path of systematic revenge. He wrote letters as though they were from her to the heads of companies where she used to work, making her sound extremely juvenile, and wrote things like how the companies were so great because she was making good money now and so on. He found out where she lived and wrote to her local post office to complain about the mail delivery, sticking it in their craw. He sent out tons of subscriptions to lesbian magazines requesting an initial copy and subscription fees; subscription postcards to a few magazines and book clubs, all of which had high subscription fees; a letter to her children's schools, complaining about the quality of education. He sent a letter to her ex-husband about how she had to sneak around the office because of this jerk who was in love with her and other things that made her look silly. He sent letters to recruiters stating that she was ready to make a career change, and even a letter to her current clients about how she'd like to work for their company. He also went in disguise to her home and dropped off a letter that stated: "You'll be sorry for what you did." He claims that he wanted to scare her so that she'd leave the office where they both worked. But he admitted, "I also want to leave because it's hard to see her."

Melanie ended up resigning from the company. As Zach said, "I thought I would feel triumph, but actually I feel empty." He later sent an anonymous letter to the woman's house, calling her shallow, immature, and heartless. Soon after, he too left the company and also found out where she was working. Not long after, he randomly interviewed at the same company she ended up with—and was considering taking the job. Scary how some things just don't end.

DETAILS, DETAILS...

One Florida man took a photo of his girlfriend while she was nude. When they broke up two years later, he posted the photo on her MySpace account—and handed out copies to friends. But he forgot about one tiny detail: The girl was only fifteen when he photographed her. So he ended up being accused of child abuse.

Personally, whenever I have felt that I was the victim of unfortunate circumstances, being treated badly, unjustly, feeling sorry for myself, wanting to lash out, to get even with my perpetrator, more often than not, I stop short of thrusting the knife or sending the angry shoe box filled with feces. I often write the nasty letter, but stop short of sending it. Somewhere, in the back of my mind, I have convinced myself that I will ultimately only do more harm to myself.

Because I played Hamlet three different times as a younger actor, perhaps my hesitation to find satisfaction in retribution has been too influenced by Hamlet's problems, learning that his father was murdered by his uncle, who subsequently married his mother. I found that Hamlet's cry for vengeance in the play was always one of the most satisfying moments of release. That one word seemed to say it all.

Sometimes it came out as an angry scream for justice, sometimes as the embodiment of a wish-fulfilling prophecy, and occasionally as a whimper or a wail denoting the recognition of something unattainable, of a lost soul in pain crying for help. As I recall, I don't think I ever found it to be the same in any two performances.

Needless to say, there have been moments in life away from Hamlet when I have wanted to throttle the person who inflicted hurt to my pride, my ego, my soul. When that happens, all of the clichés that accompany the notions of revenge come to mind, such as "Don't get mad, get even" or "Revenge is a dish best served cold," but I think the quote that strikes me as the one closest to my feelings is what Confucius said: "Before you embark on a journey of revenge, dig two graves."—Stacy Keach

So it's done. Whether or not your revenge backfired, you've reached the finish line. It might have been a long road filled with confusion, tears, and hopefully some laughs, but now you realize it's time to move on. But you're stuck, directionless, and unable to figure out which path to take. Head on over to the next chapter and check out some different takes, which may have not been your first choice but may serve you well in the long run.

Chapter 9

THE DISHES ARE DONE

> In taking revenge, a man is but even with his enemy; but in passing it over, he is superior.—Sir Francis Bacon

One of the worst realizations about this messy, adulterous breakup is that before he put his pickle into another jar, *you* waited on him hand and foot. *You* came up with the dinner plans and then executed them. *You* initiated the sexual positions. *You* spent your time buying his whole family presents for the holidays. So now what?

If things have ended between you two, it is imperative that *you* don't fall into the "rebound trap." The rebound trap is a vicious cycle of wanton behavior where you lower your standards and raise your skirt for any Joe who'll hit on you. Whether it's on the subway, in the bookstore, or at the zoo, you're looking to fill more than the empty, cavernous hole in your heart; you're also looking to fill the mental void in your head—rejection. Or you start dialing into the you-and-an-old-ex-boyfriend booty-call time. It's important to find *you* time. That means doing things by yourself in order to find yourself. It's not about *him* anymore. It's actually not about anyone else anymore. It's about *you*.

The only way that you'll move on and finally find Mr. Right after Mr. Dead Wrong is to realize what a great and strong person you've become and have always been, even if there were times when those qualities weren't so visible. Sometimes it's better to simply trust that karma will come and do its thing to those who deserve it. That way, if you can walk

away from this life-changing "affair" a bigger person, you'll have won something no court, dissolution of marriage, or revenge can afford . . . dignity and pride.

Spinning Things Right

One bride-to-be in Vermont discovered that her fiancé was having an affair. But when she learned she couldn't cancel the prepaid reservations she'd made for her wedding, she decided to go ahead with the gathering but put a different spin on the event. She converted the wedding into a charity event to benefit the Vermont Children's Aid Society and CARE; the latter organization works to empower women in developing nations. The bride-to-be still went on her honeymoon to Tahiti—with her mother.

The Power

Now, take an objective look at the situation. His suits have been incinerated, his childhood baseball card collection is sitting on top of a humidifier, and you've sent a basket of genital herpes creams to his office. In other words, you've purged him from your system. Or have you?

Reassembling the Broken Heart

One traveling exhibition was called *The Museum of Broken Relationships*. Created by a couple from Croatia who were dealing with their own breakup and who wanted to figure out how to creatively move past all their painful memories, the

(continued)

museum became a collection of trinkets and leftovers from busted-up relationships, assembled as a collection of art. There were items ranging from love letters to bikes to handcuffs to an ax that was used to hack an ex's furniture to pieces when the lover cheated on her. And the public in each city that the museum traveled to was asked to donate any object from their past heartbreak,  along with details like where they were from, how long the relationship lasted, and what this object meant. As the museum's Web site stated, "This museum allows you to get rid of things that trigger bad memories."

"In our lives, we're incredibly powerless," says David A. Sbarra of the University of Arizona. "When someone cheats on us, there's not much that we can do. Throwing the person's clothes on the curb is not going to do anything. We're going to humiliate the person, but it's only going to make us feel worse. The idea that there would be something or anything we can do that would empower us when we've been humiliated I think would be a powerful thing for people. And it's sort of like a fantasy."

Steven Hodes, MD, a physician turned metaphysician and author of the book *Meta-Physician on Call for Better Health*, explains that when you're in a relationship, you're already in a vulnerable position. So when you're hurt in that relationship, you're automatically on the losing side. But stepping back, letting time pass, and gaining perspective on the situation will allow you to pull it together and become stronger. "You can be more objective about the breakup and reframe it as something that needed to happen, or that the problem isn't necessarily with you, it's with the other person, and it allows you to heal what precipitated the feelings of revenge," says Hodes.

Taking a step back and letting these moments pass is sometimes easier said than done. Revenge is a natural reflex for many who get hurt. Raymond DiGiuseppe of St. John's University asked people in his anger groups how much they would pay in order to exact revenge and not get caught. "The bidding never starts under a hundred dollars," he says. But "people always experience the aggression that's done to them as more intense than what they do. Where does it stop? As the Bible says, 'an eye for an eye.' That's not true. They always want an eye and a half. [And then] someone has to take responsibility to say, if you strike me, I'm not going to strike you back."

Kristina Coop Gordon of the University of Tennessee brings up another scenario. In cases where a couple is trying to work things out after a betrayal, revenge "just doesn't cause damage to the partner; often, if you're ultimately going to stay together, it causes damage to [both of] them."

Revenge—on a personal level—seems to require time and planning. I never seem to have much of either. I've had the impulse, felt betrayal, etc., but then it fades away. Life

inevitably seems to catch up to [punish] the wrongdoers.—
writer Bruce Jay Friedman

Get Your Brake On

In the heat of the moment, it can be hard to foresee the consequences of revenge. DiGiuseppe reminds people that "revenge is like this brief orgasm that you pay for for the next ten years. It's like having sex and getting a woman pregnant. You're going to have a brief moment of pleasure with years of payback. There's responsibility for a long time." To put it even more simply: You may feel good for that brief sputtering moment because you made him pay, but at what cost is it to you?

Even the late Nick James of getrevengeonyourex.com, who spent hours on end helping others get revenge, said, "The only word of caution I offer when getting revenge is to know when to stop. When planning a revenge campaign, it's important to set an end date; otherwise it can drag on and on, which just leaves you bitter and twisted."

There are various ways to put the brakes on revenge. One method of gaining some perspective on the situation can be meditation. As Hodes suggests, meditation can let you "witness" your emotions, rather than become consumed by them. It's a challenging technique to master, especially when you're being bombarded by dark feelings, but it's a goal that many strive for. "It's like creating a space between yourself and your feelings, and it's a technique that allows you to face them but not be overwhelmed," Hodes says. Similar to cognitive therapy, it's about using your thinking to regulate your emotional responses.

If this type of meditation isn't cutting it, you may need a little "help" from other areas. It doesn't matter what form this help takes—whether it's professional therapy, hanging out with friends, talking to your mother, driving cross-country by your-self, chopping and dying your hair, shoving Krispy Kreme doughnuts down your throat, or spending endless hours at the gym. One of these things may be exactly what you need to yank yourself away from any thought of "him," vengeful or other-wise. Although some of these actions simply put a bandage on the true emotions bubbling underneath, they might be the per-fect way for you to get through some hellish times.

> There is no revenge so complete as forgiveness.—Josh
> Billings, American humor writer and lecturer

Forgive Him?

Some people feel that finding a way to forgive is the best way to heal. Some say being able to forgive "frees" you. But what about him? Isn't he getting off too lightly? Why doesn't he pay for what he did? Just because he cheats doesn't mean you have to be Mother Teresa.

DiGiuseppe believes that forgiving your ex can mean you're acknowledging that you were wrong, and means that "you're at the mercy of someone who may not have asked for forgiveness, may not acknowledge he's wrong." Basically, his culpability has been diminished.

> Revenge is not sweet, but bitter. To carry anger from day
> to day is to weaken your health, darken your heart, and
> miss the joy of today and the moments it composes.—
> actor Tina Louise

However, Gordon disagrees with those who see forgive-ness as negative; instead, she says forgiveness is the way to go.

"True forgiveness is not at all excusing people from responsibility. In fact, if that's the case, if the person's not responsible, then what is there to forgive?"

Steve Yoshimura of the University of Montana explains that he became involved with studying revenge by first studying forgiveness. He realized that there were limited studies on how people communicated their way through forgiveness. And when looking at situations such as infidelity, he wondered if it was really possible for people to forgive. "The problem with forgiveness is that victims can be left feeling as if the relationship is inequitable and unfair. Because if a person decides to forgive another person, in essence what they're doing is feeling angry at the person, but giving up their right to punish the person and generally accepting the person in return." But he goes on to say, "Forgiveness is definitely possible but gets easier after people had a sense of justice and fairness in their relationship. If there's any one way that offended victims in their relationship restore justice or a sense of justice and fairness, it is through revenge."

It's a toss-up when it comes to figuring out whether to go down the path of revenge—a road fraught with risks to both parties—or to stay on course as an unconditionally "forgiving" or "accepting" person. Joan Harvey, a psychologist at the University of Newcastle in the UK, stated in an article for the Newsquest Media Group, "People [exact revenge] to get a feeling of balance. . . . No matter how hurt you might have been, you can never equate that with hurting the other person by revenge . . . When you think about the revenge years later, it will also remind you of how you were hurt."

When a woman comes to me and says, I think my husband (or lover) is cheating, then I say, there's a 95 percent chance he is, so I want you to take the money you'd spend on me and pick your favorite friend with the most common sense and go out to dinner and map out a plan for what you are going to do. Usually, I end up on the phone with the woman for two or three hours hearing it all, giving advice, telling her how to make sure he's cheating (since they always have to have it hit them in the face like a pie), and telling her to respect herself as a valued person. We discuss the possible confrontation— we actually rehearse it. I don't always recommend the confrontation. Then I ask her if she wants to stay and forgive him and forget it—the European way. Or does she want to move out his things and find someone more worthy of her. Sometimes [the woman is] pregnant; it's always a mess. Especially in New York, when you toss in things like rent-controlled apartments.—Clarissa McNair, author and private investigator for Green Star Investigations

The Control

But what if you are unable to forgive? How do you deal with all of these turbulent emotions of vengeance? In our society filled with control freaks, we immediately panic when things start to get a little chaotic. "We shouldn't beat ourselves up if we have those feelings," says Dr. Steven Hodes. "As much as they may not seem to be ideal or that we shouldn't act on them, it doesn't mean we have to say, 'I'm out of control; what kind of person am I?' Just acknowledge that it's a normal human reaction, and then say, 'I'm human; I react when I'm hurt but it doesn't mean I have to go out and act on it.'"

Another way to look at things, according to Kristina Coop Gordon, is to accept "your feelings, and also accept that your partner often had a different perspective, different things [that] motivated him to whatever the betrayal was, and to come to some kind of understanding of that allows for you to have your perspective and him to have his perspective, and learn from whatever happened to lower the probability that this will happen again."

It's an ideal stance for sure, but what Hodes sees in humans is a desire for revenge that is shallower in some and deeper in others. His view on revenge, and the choices that people have to make for themselves if they're going to pursue it, is that it's always an option since it's in our nature as humans to act on it. "Justice is based on reflection, time, and consideration, where there should not be this emotional element to it. But all kinds of justice are really based on compensation of some kind for an action that's been damaging." Hodes adds that one shouldn't suppress those feelings of desiring revenge. "Recognize them as having some legitimacy. There's a reason behind why we feel what we feel, but then understand that we're not compelled to react. We need to consider what the implications of our reactions would be, and also perhaps to look at other ways of dealing with those feelings."

Bottom line, as Raymond DiGiuseppe puts it, your ex is still controlling you if you want to exact revenge on her or him. "The key is that most people who get revenge have this ruminative capacity. The other person is bad and they deserve to suffer. But in bringing them to suffer, you're spending your life thinking about them suffering and not enjoying your life."

The Cold Shoulder

Intellectually, you understand what you should do to move past him; but emotionally, you're still stuck. You just can't seem to forgive and forget. DiGiuseppe suggests that "you accept that it's going to cost you; it's time invested and you have no guarantee that you're going to hurt the person. The thing that hurts the person the most is your indifference. The most hurtful thing that you can do to anybody is ignore them."

Some of you may be shaking your heads, thinking, *There's no forgiving this jerk. Why should I ignore the schmuck who was just caught with his pants down and not give him the spanking he deserves?* Remember the saying that grandmothers, Buddhists, and kindergarten teachers are known for: Sometimes the hardest decision is the best decision to make.

Showing your ex that you're no longer suffering could be the best revenge of all. Show him that he's simply not worth the trouble, which could always add a nice dent to his ego. You learn to become a better person, not caring about continuing to hurt or humiliate him. It may be hard to do. But maybe that's why grandma Ethel, Confucius, and Mrs. Brown also wielded the old adage "That which doesn't kill you makes you stronger." Maybe not Confucius, but you catch my drift.

Live It Up

What's the best revenge? Marrying someone richer and better. There's no better revenge than success.—Vinny Parco, PI

According to DiGiuseppe, "The oddity is, living well is the best revenge. It's remarkably trite, but isn't that the only way to liberate yourself from the control of the person who hurt you?"

> They say that the ultimate revenge is success. Continue to do what you do; excel at being you with a smile on your face! Let the ex watch you succeed at all you do. That is the best revenge.—actor Shar Jackson

Princess Diana received rave reviews when she showed up looking more elegant and beautiful than ever after it became publicly known that Charles still had a thing with Camilla.

When Christie Brinkley split with her cheating ex, the New York *Daily News* described her courtroom attire as "revenge dressing worthy of a runway."

After being pitted out of Brad's life, Jennifer Aniston was photographed all over Hawaii in a tiny bikini that got everyone talking about her gorgeous figure.

Taking a page from these women's lives may keep you from falling into a trap that could cause dire consequences. Learn that you are the most important person in your life, and that sitting home alone crying over "him" will only leave you with exactly that: sitting home alone crying over him. But if you can muster the courage to get out there, take care of yourself, work hard, and ideally catapult whatever career or following relationship you have to success, you will succeed in the ultimate revenge of "moving on." And be sure that "he" will somehow find out one day that you are successful and happy—at which point, hopefully, you won't even care if he knows it or not.

Which Path?

You have the choice and the power. Stay in your misery or move on. It's your life, and no one can make those decisions for you. If you're still not sure which way to go, it can be helpful to heed the advice of Alfred, Lord Tennyson, who once said, "It's better to have loved and lost, than to have never loved at all," even if it turned out to be with the wrong guy, one who didn't deserve your love at all.

It's also helpful to remind yourself that when a guy cheats once, there's a good chance he'll cheat again, no matter whom he's with. Or if he treats you badly, he's usually not going to get much better. So you should probably feel sorry for his new victim, not necessarily vindictive.

How Things Come Back Around

"Faye" used to date "Mike," who would shower her with books, inscribing them with sweet and thoughtful words. He was a writer, but paid the bills by working in the mailroom at

(continued)

an ad agency—the same agency where Faye was an account executive.

When they broke up, Faye dated a guy named "Tom." He also liked books, and often borrowed hers. She liked him, but when he kept showing up drunk in the middle of the night, she started breaking up with him. Each time, he'd win her back…till things eventually ended.

Somehow, Faye and Mike reconnected and hung out once in a while. He was working in a different ad agency and one of his female coworkers brought a book to the office. He loved the author and asked to see the book. When he opened it, he found an inscription there, in his very own handwriting. Turns out, his coworker was now dating Tom, who had borrowed the book from Faye and never returned it. Mike took the book and returned it to Faye.

Faye now has the book and keeps it, saying, "The book traveled a far way to get back to me, through two different relationships. The inscription from Mike said that he wanted me to read the book, as he was inspired by strong women. What I got out of it was that both relationships ended for a reason and I was stronger for it."

In the end, figuring out what makes you happy is truly the only way to move on past that lying, cheating bastard. However you reach that point—whether by shipping everything he owns to a refugee camp in Africa or by accepting the fact that he'll always be one flighty Peter Pan (and no woman—not even you—will change him!) or by forgiving him for having a threesome with the babysitter and her sister—is up to you. Whatever path you choose should be what most satisfies you in the end. And for some, devouring *The Down and Dirty Dish on Revenge* may hit the spot!

Down and Dirty Flicks

WICKED FILMS ON
(PASSIONATE) REVENGE

As far as revenge goes in films, I have to say nothing is more satisfying. I have two favorite examples and I can't decide between them. First is the infamous scene in *Grease* where Sandy shows up at the carnival in her tight, sassy (and seriously outdated now) greaser outfit and blows all the men away. After Danny treats her like just another floozy, your heart just jumps when you hear the song "Better Shape Up" and the camera pans up her tight leather pants to her curly blond 'fro. It's so awesome, it makes me blush.

A more serious revenge story that rocks my world is Braveheart. After falling for and marrying the girl of his dreams, [the hero] finds her with her throat slashed. This sparks a historic massacre of the British. Even though he hardly knew the chick, it is completely believable to the viewers that he would spend his life avenging her death.—actor Melissa Joan Hart on her favorite revenge movies

Here's a rundown of some down and dirty flicks that focus on passionate revenge. Raymond DiGiuseppe of St. John's University believes that films, especially the movies of contemporary America, have changed the way revenge is perceived. "I think from *Orestes* through most of the twentieth century, the theme was 'revenge gets you in trouble.' Achilles doesn't make out good with revenge. There's the message from *Orestes*, that we're civilized because we overcome our urges for revenge. I would argue that it's present-day movies that have changed that literary theme. Watch Denzel Washington in *Man on Fire*; watch *Kill Bill*. Revenge is glorified now, and it really wasn't in the past."

So stack your Netflix queue with these classics in revenge cinema, butter up some popcorn, kick back, and enjoy the show. (Warning: Spoiler Alert! The following summaries may give away the plot!)

Thérèse Raquin (1953)

A classic tale. Thérèse is unhappily married and soon falls for another man. They decide to escape together, but not without her lover having to kill Thérèse's husband. Her mother-in-law, who suffered a stroke upon hearing about the death of her son, stares at Thérèse with accusing eyes, causing her to go insane with grief. On top of it, Thérèse and her lover get blackmailed by someone who saw the whole crime go down. Can you say "clusterfuck"?

Love(less) Letters

Did Madeleine Smith, daughter of a wealthy family, poison her lover, Emile, a clerk at a seed warehouse in 1850s Scotland? She and Emile had had a romance that involved some hot and steamy letter-writing. But when she tried to dump him for some upper-class guy from Glasgow that her parents set her up with (her parents didn't know about Emile), he was mad and decided he wouldn't acknowledge her request to return all the letters she wrote to him. Those earnest letters were one of the most extreme kinds of blackmail one could have during those days, and could cause quite a scandal if leaked to the public. Not too much later, Emile was found dead from arsenic poisoning. But at the end of a spectacular trial, during

(continued)

which she charmed everyone with her composure, Madeleine was found not guilty. The tale has inspired many books, plays, documentaries, and films (such as the 1952 film *Madeline*).

Dial M for Murder (1954)

Ex–tennis pro Tony Wendice wants to get back at his wife (played by Grace Kelly) for having had an affair the year before, although he never confronted her about it. He blackmails an old college friend to murder her. Even when things don't go quite as planned, he does seem to have the ball in his court . . . if only for a while.

A Perfect Murder (1998)

In this spin-off of *Dial M for Murder*, Steven (Michael Douglas) hires a hit man to wipe out his wife, Emily (Gwyneth Paltrow). But things get complicated when the murderer turns out to be Emily's lover.

Les Diaboliques (The Devils, 1955)

A wife and her husband's lover decide to exact revenge on the man they share, a boarding-school headmaster who treats both of them like shit. But when they throw his dead body into the pool, and the body later vanishes, the two women start to unravel, unable to comprehend all of the mysterious events that begin unfolding around them.

Carrie (1976)

Nobody pours pig's blood on Carrie White at the homecoming dance! Nobody! Die!!!

Too Emotional

Former model and nightclub hostess Ruth Ellis was the last woman hanged in Britain in the twentieth century (in 1955). She and her lover, race car driver David Blakely, had one testy relationship, with him supposedly having countless female lovers, and her having affairs as well. Their jealousy instigated fights, money problems, and reportedly even a miscarriage (after Blakely supposedly punched her in the stomach). When Blakely finally left her, she couldn't handle it and she shot him in broad daylight on a street and even waited for the police to arrive at the scene. The case inspired the 1985 movie *Dance with a Stranger*, starring Miranda Richardson.

Unfaithfully Yours (1984)

Dudley Moore plays a conductor who orchestrates a revenge scheme to get back at his younger wife and his close friend, with whom he thinks she's having an affair. While he knows how to put notes together onstage, things go awry offstage when he realizes he may have mistaken what's fact and fiction.

Fatal Attraction (1987)

You think wives are the only ones who feel scorned? Think again and watch as a jilted Alex (Glenn Close) takes her revenge on Dan (Michael Douglas) in a truly terrifying way. Rabbit stew, anyone?

Only Room for Two of Us

Carolyn Warmus had a real-life fatal attraction. In 1989, the wealthy heiress killed her lover's wife, shooting her nine times at close range. She was given twenty-five years to life, and will be eligible for parole in 2017, at the age of fifty-three.

Women on the Verge of a Nervous Breakdown (1988)

A woman is pissed off that her married lover is trying to end things with her. When she decides to confront him, she instead finds herself hanging out with his wife and son. Then another friend joins them in her apartment (in which the entire film takes place), and it turns out that her boyfriend's lawyer is the main character's married lover's *other* lover! Did you get all that? Well, you'll just have to see this hilarious film. A burned bed and laced gazpacho are just a few of the adventures these women go through, all in one homey atmosphere.

Movie Stars Outside Their Movies

Lana Turner was a true movie star. After four marriages, and one daughter, Cheryl, she met Johnny Stompanato, a gangster. Despite his "career," they began a romance. But that didn't mean she wanted to be seen in public with him; she even refused to attend the Oscars with him when she was nominated. He was so angry he wasn't allowed to be her escort that he bloodied and bruised her to make sure she wouldn't go stag. Turner found herself stuck in this relationship, unable to get out of it without screwing up her career.

So her daughter took matters into her own hands. At the age of fourteen, she stabbed Johnny Stompanato to death when he and Turner were fighting, and supposedly, Turner's acting performance in court saved her daughter from a future behind bars.

The War of the Roses (1989)

Barbara Rose (Kathleen Turner) and Oliver Rose (Michael Douglas) take the concept of a nasty divorce to a whole new level. From pissed-on fish to heel-less shoes to hanging on chandeliers, the Roses send the custody battle for their house into oblivion. Cringe in delight when she bites his noodle.

She-Devil (1989)

When a heavyset woman (Roseanne Barr) loses her husband to a beautiful novelist, she turns into a She-Devil and makes him pay wickedly.

Double Heat

In the early 1900s, Ruth Snyder convinced her lover, Judd Gray, that her husband treated her like shit and she wanted freedom. So what's a guy to do but help her murder the op-

(continued)

pressor? There was even the bonus of a life-insurance policy. They attempted to kill Ruth's husband several times, and they finally succeeded. But they were eventually caught . . . and each ended up blaming the other for what happened. They were both executed, with Ruth being the first woman ever to die in Sing Sing's electric chair. Their story of lust, greed, and murder has inspired films such as *Double Indemnity* and *Body Heat*.

Sea of Love (1989)

A serial killer is using personal ads to meet his victims. Burned-out NYPD detective Frank (Al Pacino) is trying to figure out who it is, but he gets thrown a curve when he falls for Helen (Ellen Barkin), who also happens to be the number one suspect in the case. The revenge twist is indeed twisted.

Dangerous Liaisons (1988) and Valmont (1989)

In these films, both based on the novel *Dangerous Liaisons* by Pierre Ambroise Francois Choderlos de Laclos, the marquise de Merteuil is one scorned and bitter mistress. So when she finds out that her lover, Gercourt, is about to marry her cousin's teenage daughter, she plots a vengeful scheme. Knowing about Gercourt's wish to keep his future wife pure, Merteuil spins Valmont into her conspiracy web to make sure the bride-to-be is properly deflowered—only things don't quite turn out as she had planned.

Playboy

Dorothy Stratten was a hot *Playboy* centerfold, who was tragically killed by her ex, hustler Paul Snider, when she was just twenty years old. She had already left him for director Peter Bogdanovich but didn't know that Snider had a PI following her every move. When Snider convinced her to come to his apartment, he shot her and then allegedly sodomized her dead body before turning the gun on himself. This case became the subject of countless films and TV movies, such as *Death of a Centerfold* (1981) and *Star 80* (1983). Bogdanovich later married Dorothy's younger sister, Louise.

Presumed Innocent (1990)

DA Rusty Sabich (Harrison Ford) is charged with killing his mistress. He goes on a mission to find out who really did it, not realizing just how close he is to the killer. "Destroyer is destroyed."

Revenge (1990)

Some husbands don't know how to forgive their wives for falling for another man, even if they aren't the most faithful hubbies themselves. A jealous Mexican crime lord (Anthony Quinn) makes sure his wife (Madeleine Stowe) and her lover—his friend—(Kevin Costner) get a serious beating. He even makes sure his wife continues to suffer, by tossing her into a whorehouse, while the Costner character sets out to seek his own revenge.

I Love You to Death (1990)

Kevin Kline portrays a hilarious Italian Casanova, Joey, who is a pizza man by day and a cheating husband by night. He's insatiable. When his enamored wife finally catches wind of his "other" life outside the pizza parlor, she decides to have him killed. But this proves to be ridiculously difficult. After surviving several attempts on his life—including his wife's own sleeping pill–spaghetti concoction—Joey proves that nothing can kill his charm.

Thelma and Louise (1991)

One helluva revenge road trip.

Obsession

Betty Broderick was so obsessed and bitter about her divorce from her ex-husband (and father of her four children) and his marrying another woman who was years younger, she shot them both, killing them while they slept. Her story inspired two Lifetime TV movies, *A Woman Scorned: The Betty Broderick Story* and *Her Final Fury: Betty Broderick, the Last Chapter*, both in 1992.

Waiting to Exhale (1995)

Four women bond, trying to figure out if they can be happy with or without men. Although it's not a film entirely devoted to vengeance, Angela Bassett's character, Bernadine, makes it revenge-worthy by her fantastic wardrobe-trashing scene, where she takes all of her husband's clothes and lights them on fire *inside* his car. She also has a yard sale, at which she sells all of his stuff for $1 an item—quite a bargain for a pair of skis.

Thin Line Between Love and Hate (1996)

Darnell (Martin Lawrence) messes with the wrong rich woman. He uses the classic phrase "I love you" just to get in her pants, and then pays for it dearly.

The Politician's Wife (1995)

This juicy, award-winning UK TV miniseries is centered on one wife's systematic and calculating revenge on her husband, a government minister in the British parliament, who has been visiting a call girl. With the help of her hubby's aide, a gay man disgusted by his boss's homophobia, the wife not only puts on a brave face but manages to twist and turn his career upside-down. Felicity Huffman is reportedly set to star in the U.S. remake of the series into a feature film in 2010.

The First Wives Club (1996)

Diane Keaton, Bette Midler, and Goldie Hawn play middle-aged women dangerously close to the edge after they are dumped by their husbands for younger models. They decide to get revenge by hitting their exes where it hurts—in the wallet! White-collar revenge at its best.

All the Revenge That's Fit to Watch

Heartburn was Nora Ephron's semiautobiographical novel about her marriage to a cheater, *Washington Post* reporter Carl Bernstein. The *Chicago Tribune* reviewed the book, saying, "proof that writing well is the best revenge." Bonus was she also got to write it as a screenplay, which was adapted into a Mike Nichols movie, starring Jack Nicholson and Meryl Streep.

Addicted to Love (1997)

Maggie (Meg Ryan) and Sam (Matthew Broderick) find themselves obsessively spying and plotting revenge against their ex-lovers, who are now together. From lipsticked monkeys to water guns filled with perfume to roaches set free, they discover what true love is all about.

Unfaithful (2002)

Connie Sumner has the idyllic life: adoring husband, great home, perfect son. But when she literally bumps into a hot Frenchman in SoHo, a steamy, secret affair challenges her marriage and the decisions of her husband. Snow globes, anyone?

Kill Bill: Vol. 1 (2003) and Kill Bill: Vol. 2 (2004)

Shot and left for dead, the bride (Uma Thurman) gets some kick-ass revenge.

No matter how many revenge stories I consider, the process of elimination always filters down to *Kill Bill*. This is an amazing collection of multiple revenge stories tied together by a single thread.—musician and producer Nile Rodgers

My Super-Ex Girlfriend (2006)

Jenny (Uma Thurman) has supernatural powers and makes her ex's, Luke Wilson's, life a living hell when he dumps her. Break up with a super-chick at your own risk!

The Break-Up (2006)

Brooke (Jennifer Aniston) and her ex (Vince Vaughn) decide to torture each other during their breakup by continuing to live together in the same apartment. But do they really want to get rid of each other or are they simply trying to win each other back? Aniston struts one hell of a revenge nude scene.

John Tucker Must Die (2006)

Three ex-girlfriends decide to exact revenge on their high-school boyfriend (whom they were all dating at the same time). They get him to fall for "the new girl" in school so that they can shatter his heart into tiny little pieces.

Talk About Casting a Spell . . . on TV

On the TV show *Buffy the Vampire Slayer*, Anyanka was a Vengeance Demon and the patron saint of scorned women. She had a talent for bringing "ruin to the heads of unfaithful men," saying, "I brought forth destruction and chaos for the pleasure of the lower beings." It all "started" back in 880 A.D. when she fell in love with a Viking warrior, Olaf, who cheated on her with a barmaid. Aud (Anyanka's birth name) was so peeved, she turned him into a troll. The demon D'Hoffryn caught wind of this and transformed her into an immortal vengeance demon. That basically meant that Anyanka was able to grant wishes (think: boils on the penis) for women who want to get back at men who had hurt and/or betrayed them by using a "special" necklace (her power center).

45 (2006)

Mila Jovovich plays Kat, a hot chick who lives under the thumb of her boyfriend, Big Al. But Al's number two also has the hots for her and will do anything for her. So when Kat decides to get revenge on her abusive boyfriend, she's got more planned than just falling in love again, even with a loyal henchman.

The New Lolita

The story of the Long Island Lolita was one that didn't end in death, but it sure flirted with it. In 1992, seventeen-year-old Amy Fisher was involved with auto mechanic Joey Buttafuoco, who was married and twenty-one years her senior. Amy wanted Joey all to herself, so one day she went to his home and shot Buttafuoco's wife, Mary Jo, in the face, partially paralyzing her. Mary Jo not only survived, but even stood by her husband, who served six months for statutory rape. The case captivated the nation, and Amy and Joey became household names, with several movies made about them. Amy was released after seven years, and Mary Jo managed to find a way to forgive her assailant. But in 2003, Mary Jo and Joey finally divorced. And in 2007, Amy and Joey supposedly left their respected spouses on the same day, saying they were moving in together. Rumor had it that they were actually preparing for a possible reality TV show.

The Painted Veil (1934, 2006)

When Englishman Dr. Walter Fane discovers his wife's infidelity, he takes revenge on her by forcing her to go with him to rural China to deal with a deadly cholera epidemic. This loveless marriage finds heart and meaning—and in the end, the revenge actually brings the two closer together.

Crazy Love (2007)

A lot can be said about the infamous couple Burt and Linda Pagach, whose lives were documented in this film. But one thing's for sure: They've made their marriage last. They started dating in the 1950s, when Burt was still married. But since he wouldn't get a divorce, Linda moved on and got engaged to someone else. This pissed off Burt so much that he arranged for someone to throw acid in Linda's face. Linda was left blind and disfigured. Yet love sometimes conquers all, and Linda waited fourteen years for Burt to get out of jail before marrying him. They currently live together in Queens, New York, and are constantly dealing with their demons and Burt's continuing penchant for affairs.

Over Her Dead Body (2008)

When Kate (Eva Longoria) is killed while preparing for her wedding, she still can't give up her fiancé—even from the grave. So when he starts dating a psychic who speaks with the dead, Kate lets her know loud and clear to stay away from the man who should have been hers.

One Sticky Flush

One movie in the making (and possibly released by the time you read this book) is *Serious Moonlight,* starring Meg Ryan, about a woman who duct tapes her husband to the toilet when she finds out he's about to leave her for another woman. She does it in the hopes that he'll change his mind and stay with her . . . but things don't quite go according to plan when the house gets robbed.

Down and Dirty Playlist

ROCKIN' (PASSIONATE) REVENGE SONGS

These songs are about breaking up. But gone are the days when the lyrics were all about crying oneself to sleep, dreaming "he" (or "she") would return. Now it's about standing up for yourself, getting even, and moving on.

The sections are divided up between rocker men and women since both sides do get hurt and desire a little retribution. Sometimes they react a little differently—and sometimes they don't.

Here's a taste from a few women who decided to kick some lyrical ass:

Kaki King, "Life Being What It Is" (from her album *Dreaming of Revenge*)
"We all dream of revenge."

Hilary Duff, "Dignity"
"Where's your dignity? / I think you lost it in the Hollywood Hills."

Also, Duff claims that her song "Hated" was not meant to be about Lindsay Lohan, who dated Duff's ex Aaron Carter. Some lyrics: *"You say your boyfriend's sweet and kind / But you've still got your eyes on mine."*

Fiona Apple, "Limp"
"It won't be long till you'll be / Lying limp in your own hand."

Apple is reported to have said that she wrote many of her songs "to get revenge on whoever I was angry with at the time."

Alanis Morissette, "You Oughta Know"
"And every time I scratch my nails down someone else's back / I hope you feel it!"

In *Interview* magazine, Morissette is quoted as saying, "I spoke to this person after having been broken up with him for a year. I was still very much affected, and very perturbed because I thought, God, a year has gone by. I guess I was hoping during that year that I had consciously begun to move on. So I wrote down everything that I was feeling, just so I could get down to exactly what I felt."

Mary J. Blige, "Not Gon' Cry"

"Wasted my years a fool of a wife / I shoulda have left your ass a long time ago."

Dixie Chicks, "Goodbye Earl"

"And it didn't take long to decide / That Earl had to die."

Carrie Underwood, "Before He Cheats"

"That I dug my key into the side of his pretty little souped-up 4 wheel drive."

In a *People* magazine interview, Underwood said that she wasn't really in touch with her exes from her pre–*American Idol* days. But she does admit that her fame has given her the upper hand: "[It's like,] well, you wish you would have stayed with me, huh?"

Madonna, "You'll See"

"I have truth on my side, / You only have deceit."

Kelly Clarkson, "Never Again"

"You'll die together but alone."

Lily Allen, "Smile"

"Now you're calling me up on the phone . . . / Yeah it makes me smile."

This song was allegedly about Allen's ex-boyfriend DJ Lester Lloyd's writing a tell-all about their relationship in the Sunday paper. In the video for the song, she gets some guys to beat up a guy, trash his apartment, and ruin his vinyl records. To top it off, she comforts him after all this . . . only to then slip him a bunch of laxatives. In real life? Aside from the song, word is, she supposedly got revenge by sleeping with all of his friends.

Lily Allen, "Not Big"

"I'm gonna tell the world you're rubbish in bed now."

Beyoncé, "Irreplaceable"

"I can have another you by tomorrow."

Madison Avenue, "Who the Hell Are You"

"You won't be smiling by the time I'm through with you."

P J Harvey, "Rid of Me"

"I'll make you lick my injuries."

Alicia Bridges, "I Love the Nightlife"

"You can love them all and when you're through / Maybe that'll make, huh, a man out of you."

Disco revenge!

Mandy Moore, "Looking Forward to Looking Back"

"The burns on my fingers were all that was left of the spark."

(This song was reportedly about Zach Braff, who supposedly cheated on her.)

Ashanti, "The Way I Love You"

"I found out we were living a lie."

While the words are not so vengeful, the video for this song is. It starts off with a bloody knife, a dead body, an ambulance, and Ashanti looking very guilty in a tub full of water—the same tub that is later filled with her boyfriend's bloody corpse. On top of this gruesome video, an eerie viral campaign promoted the album, where people could send "death threats" (or "Gotcha-Grams") anonymously, with a fictitious detective stating that a jealous lover was on the loose to get even with you. There was even a blood scrawl personalized in the "victim's" name: "X will die." The campaign was quickly cancelled for obvious reasons—like, scaring the hell out of anyone who got the seemingly real threat.

> She Wants Revenge—A band whose name speaks for itself.

To show the differences but overall similarities of how men can also feel love's bites—and want to bite back. Here's what some men have written about hurt and rage:

Justin Timberlake, "Cry Me a River"

"Your bridges were burned, and now it's your turn / To cry, cry me a river."

The song was supposedly inspired by his breakup with Britney Spears. It was even accompanied by a music video where Timberlake busts into what's supposed to be Spears's home, swaps tongues with another woman, and films it.

Bob Dylan, "Don't Think Twice, It's All Right"
"You just kinda wasted my precious time."

Bob Dylan, "Idiot Wind"
". . . You're an idiot, babe."

ABC, "Valentine's Day"
"If you gave me a pound for the moments I missed . . . / I'd be a millionaire."

The Police, "Can't Stand Losing You"
"But you'll be sorry when I'm dead / And all this guilt will be on your head."

Ben Folds Five, "Song for the Dumped"
"Give me my money back / you bitch."

Eminem, "Kim"
"But not for him to take my place, are you out your mind?"

James Brown, "The Payback"
"Revenge! I'm mad (the big payback)."

The Eagles, "Already Gone"
"So oftentimes it happens that we live our lives in chains / And we never even know we have the key."

Eamon, "Fuck It (I Don't Want You Back)"

"Fuck you, you ho, I don't want you back."

Simply put.

A Snowy Murder

Singer and actress Claudine Longet and her boyfriend, professional skier Spider Sabich, were a beautiful celebrity couple in the 1970s. They were living a dream existence together with Claudine's three children until rumors started flying that Spider wanted her out of his house. In the heat of an argument, Spider was shot and killed. Claudine claimed he accidentally shot himself while showing her a gun. She got off easy: She was convicted of criminal negligence, a misdemeanor, and sentenced to pay a small fine and spend thirty days in jail. After she finished doing her time, she vacationed with her married defense lawyer, waited for him to get a divorce, and married him herself. But the Sabich family sued her, settling for a large amount of money and Claudine's agreeing never to write or tell her story.

This case inspired the song "Claudine," by Mick Jagger. It was cut from the 1980 Rolling Stones album, *Emotional Rescue*, to avoid potential libel.

Saturday Night Live had a skit called "Claudine Longet Invitational Ski Shoot." It featured a skier barreling down a mountain, while gunfire went off and an announcer could be heard saying, "Oh! He has been accidentally shot by Claudine Longet."